CROSSING OVER

Stories

CROSSING OVER

Stories of Asian Refugee Christians

James Calvin Schaap

Dordt College Press

Cover design by Shar Dokter Alsum

This project is made possible through a grant from the Calvin Institute of Christian Worship, Grand Rapids, Michigan, with funds provided by Lilly Endowment Inc.

Printed in the United States of America.

Dordt College Press   www.dordt.edu/dordt_press
498 Fourth Avenue NE
Sioux Center, Iowa 51250
United States of America
ISBN: 0-932914-67-5

The Library of Congress Cataloging-in-Publication Data
is on file with the Library of Congress, Washington, D.C.

Library of Congress Control Number: 2006929816

Contents

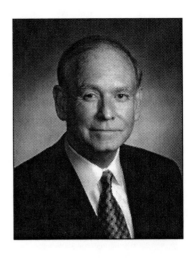

Robert E. Ray

....

Governor of the state of Iowa
1969–1983

Preface

In 1979, my wife Billie and I visited refugee camps in Thailand, including one through which most Laotians and Tai Dam would pass while en route to resettlement somewhere else in the world.

We were greeted with incredible warmth, including signs of welcome and cheers. Then, we were led by some of the refugee elders to a small thatched-roof hut that served as the camp office. The refugees said they wanted to show us the map of what came across, in translation, as their "promised land." We didn't know what to expect.

As they ushered us into this small, flimsy building, suddenly, there it was before our eyes, affixed to the unstable wall: the Iowa Department of Transportation official state map, and all across that map pins with red and blue heads were stuck, each one signifying where a Tai Dam or Lao family was already resettled, each one signifying where an Iowa family, church, or organization had opened their hearts and homes to welcome a refugee family and help them begin new lives in freedom.

The refugees at that camp in Thailand had but one impassioned plea to us that day: "Please, let us come to Iowa." The stories that had been sent back to their camp from relatives who had preceded them were filled with accounts of love and generosity, so many that everyone wanted to replicate this experience.

I am pleased to say that, just like the pioneers a hundred years before, virtually all of these refugees overcame great obstacles, and almost all made it to Iowa. And I am also pleased to say that Iowans continued to welcome these newest settlers: be they Vietnamese, Cambodian, Lao, or Tai Dam.

These refugees have paid us back many times over by becoming productive and committed members of communities all across our state and region. In *Crossing Over,* James Schaap is providing an invaluable record of how nine of these refugees have made this transition. These stories are powerful accounts of incredible physical and spiritual journeys and of a new chapter in Iowa's humanitarian heritage, as well as that of America itself.

In April of 2005, I had an experience that brought home to me just how powerful that humanitarian legacy can be. At the Hoover-Wallace Dinner in Des Moines, an eighteen-year-old ethnic Asian woman brought the audience to tears as she recounted how she had been born in a refugee camp in Thailand, her family uncertain of the future. She then described how, thanks to an Iowa community that took them in, she had just graduated from high school and was on her way to Iowa State University on a scholarship.

That dinner ended with the singing of the Iowa Corn Song, also led by a refugee woman who had built a family and career here. As she sang, I looked around the room and saw people of all races and religions, refugees and native born, standing together to sing the words that united us all and that reflected the new identity all of these refugees could now proclaim.

There could be no more clear indication that they had indeed "crossed over" and become citizens of this land.

....

....

On the Trail of the Spirit

It's been a joy to write these stories, and it's been a blessing to hear them. Each of them comes from an interview of three hours or more, a process that almost always required a translator. Three hours is a lot of talking, a lot of audiotape. But most people never have the occasion to tell their stories, and when they do, they too, find it a joy; whatever reticence they feel initially somehow fades, nervousness flattens, and the construction begins. I say *construction* because our own stories, no matter how well we know them or how deeply we feel them, tend to surface unassembled. That may be why people finally appreciate the experience — they find themselves piecing together fragments into a whole, into an extended narrative with a beginning and at least something of an end.

Each of these interviews was a great experience. Let me explain by way of a particular moment with Dokmai Vongphakdy. She had been talking about her job at Tyson's, the giant meat packer, where she, like so many of her friends, stood each day, knife in hand, making a cut or two at the chunks of shoulder or brisket coming down the line. Gently, through the translator, I offered her the idea that lots of Americans (and I pointed at myself) wouldn't care much for a job like hers. I asked her if she'd tell me what she thought of doing this work.

Picture this conversation going through the translator. Dokmai answers quickly once the translator gives her my question. Then he turns to me. "She likes her job there very much," he says.

"Could she tell me why?" I say, because I honestly can't understand her affection.

Once more, the translator gives her my question. Dokmai speaks again, going on longer this time, and then smiles. The translator grins and turns to me. "Because in Laos she was the one who had to do *all* the butchering," he says.

Before my eyes, an image appears—the entire bloody carcass of a water buffalo, Dokmai standing there alone before it with something like a machete.

I have no idea if that image is accurate, but her answer was shocking; not only was it perfectly understandable, it was embarrassing, exposing my own naiveté. What's more, it opened a window to issues raised by immigration, in my neighborhood and yours, and really around the world. To her, cutting meat at Tyson's is a great job.

I'm nearly sixty years old, but I thank God for that answer and for what I've learned through the stories these people tell, because each of them offered me an opportunity to grow. They were a blessing and a joy to me.

For the most part, the trajectories of these stories, as you might expect, are very much alike, differing only in degree. Take the matter of coming to a faith in Jesus Christ. Each story begins in some form of one of the traditional Lao religions, but ends in a soul-felt pledge to the Creator of heaven and earth and Jesus Christ, his Son.

But each story is as unique as each of us is. Sawan believed the promise of the gospel the very first time he heard it—even though today he'll tell you he didn't understand much at all. Keo didn't and wouldn't listen to those promises, until the time came when he could no longer make fun of the Christian faith. A guitar-toting evangelist on a motorcycle set a child-hood memory in Sone that didn't blossom for years. While escaping from Laos, Dokmai prayed fervently the whole time she was crossing the Mekong River; only today does she know to whom she addressed all those passionate petitions.

Eventually, however, they all listened to God's promise, and, by his grace, they all came to believe. That, of course, is the miracle of faith, and to that miracle these stories — and their tellers — give astonishing testimony.

One chapter in all of these stories prompts them all to giggle, even laugh aloud. I noticed it early on in the interviews, but it became most discernable when I listened to Sawan's story, told in the presence of his new wife, as well as both Pastor Khay and Pastor Sone. Sawan was telling me how, in those first years here, some of his friends had taken advantage of church people. He told me how they'd smiled their way into the good graces of their well-meaning hosts, then, more than once, had taken the goods and run. When he told that story in his own language, his wife, his pastor, and Khay all roared with laughter. They thought that the shenanigans were a real hoot.

> **Eventually, however, they all listened to God's promise, and, by his grace, they all came to believe. That, of course, is the miracle of faith. . . .**

At first, their hoodwinking of believers didn't seem all that hilarious to me. I'd heard the story told from the other side, too, of course — how some of the volunteers, early on, their hearts filled with righteous intentions, felt betrayed once it seemed that all of the work went nowhere.

It was their hosts — the church volunteers — who remarked (and who would never forget) how helpless the refugees were when they arrived in a climate and culture that looked and felt absolutely nothing like home. "Like babies who could walk," one of the volunteers told me. Everything, from tile floors to stop signs, was a baffling new experience.

The mother of a friend of mine immigrated to North America after the Second World War. She once told her son that her greatest sadness in leaving the culture of her birth was the loss of humor; her limited abilities with a new language wouldn't allow the latitude required for word play and silliness. Imagine being cut off from something as crucial as a laugh.

Some immigrants see themselves behind a wall that cannot be broken down, climbed over, or even dug under, a wall that separates them from the active life going on all around them. Picture yourself walking through a Super Wal-Mart and seeing nothing familiar. Imagine trying to read road signs in Laos or Thailand. If you know that someone has to help you walk through every hour of every day, it must be humiliating, like being "a baby who could walk."

Now, imagine the joy in being able, just once, to get a leg up on others. Imagine the kick it must be to manipulate those very people—no matter how kind or loving—who know so much more than you do and without whose aid you are really powerless.

That laughter arises from the need we all have for human dignity, from a spirit that despises being dependent as much as it longs to be free. Conning others—even those who want to help you—may not be Boy Scout behavior, but it's understandable, and so is their laughter when they remember those few freeing moments in the earliest weeks of their lives in this new country.

When I say it was a joy and blessing to do these stories, what I mean is that, in the process, these individuals helped me understand them, and also us, and even me. I now know more about Laos and Thailand and about the problems immigrant people face in a new world. I know more about the verifiable differences the Christian faith makes in the lives of believers. And yet I also understand more vividly how our human nature is similar, no matter the color of our skin or the nature of our faith. Asian-American or not, you'll be moved, I hope, by the humanity of these stories.

But these stories are not circumscribed by the here and now, and neither are they finished. These are all timeless stories, as eternal as all of ours are. Listening to—and then writing— them has been a blessing because I've been taken, arrested, in altogether new ways, by the miracles of God through the Holy Spirit, impressed anew by the amazing mystery of what he does. When I consider the people whose stories I heard, I am amazed at how impossible it is for any of us to predict the effects of the gospel of Jesus Christ on men and women and children of any race or background. One can't help but ask an obvious question: why are *these* folks trusting in God today, but not so many others who also heard the same promises and were beneficiaries of the same acts of kindness? What makes the Christian faith matter eternally in some people's hearts and lives—and not in others'?

The more I listen, the more sure I am that God is God, and we are not. The more I hear, the more confident I am that his ways are eternal, forever beyond our reach. That he loves us, all of us—that *this God loves us*—is the miracle we all need to celebrate, daily, and even hourly. That is a lesson I've learned anew.

I'm more sure now that John Milton was attempting the unachievable when, in *Paradise Lost,* he begged divine help to "assert th' Eternal Providence, / And justify the ways of God to men." God's ways, or so it seems to me, are beyond us; we have all we can do simply to trace the paths of our lives and rejoice in our timeless destinies. The greatest lesson for the storyteller here is, before God, a lesson in humility—and for that lesson, too, I am thankful.

My hope—and prayer—is that these stories will strengthen all who read them, no matter what their color, in the knowledge of God first of all, but second—and like unto it—in the understanding we gain of those we live beside and of our very selves.

May the lives of these good folks—their sadness and their joys, their newfound delight in our Lord—prompt our continual thanksgiving to God the Father; to his Son our faithful Savior, Jesus Christ; and to the Holy Spirit, who leaves the most remarkable trails by orchestrating the miracle of grace within each of us. May we all give thanks for God's love, no matter what our color or country of origin, both now and forevermore.

James Calvin Schaap
Sioux Center, Iowa
August 2005

....

KHAY BACCAM AND ADRIANNA DOKTER

....

A Story Without End

Believers would say that this story, like all others, begins somewhere in the tapestry of eternal cause-and-effect, in divine territory that not one of us can understand but that all of us can experience. It begins in the mystery of eternal love that is well beyond the limitations of time and space. Maybe the easiest way of saying it, for those who believe, is that this story begins in the whole counsel of God, in God's eternal plan.

But none of us are privy to that counsel, so for purposes of our limited human understanding, we need to start elsewhere. Given what we can grasp, it might be helpful to think that this story begins at the moment the Vietnam War ended, with the fall of Saigon in April 1975.

Most Americans who can remember the end of that war would likely rather forget the images — the helicopters leaving government building rooftops where dozens of Vietnamese loyalists wave frantically, hoping and praying for a last-minute escape that will not come.

Scene two of this story takes place almost immediately thereafter in nearby Laos, where the American retreat made life extremely dangerous for those Laotian people who were, on the basis of their association with American troops, the enemy of the victors. Some of those Laotians were Tai Dam, a people who had fled to Laos a quarter-century earlier, when North Vietnam was taken over by a communist government. More than 1,200 of the Tai Dam people, seeking asylum, crossed from Laos into Thailand just two weeks after the fall of Saigon.

A former United States government official named Arthur Crisfield, who had worked with the Tai Dam, took it upon himself to write to thirty state governors with a plea to help the Tai Dam people, a separate nation within the many nations of Southeast Asia. What he wanted for the Tai Dam was not only deliverance from their oppressors, but also a place where they could immigrate in significant numbers, a place for them

Scene two of this story takes place almost immediately thereafter in nearby Laos, where the American retreat made life extremely dangerous for those Laotian people ....

to live and then grow slowly into a cultural milieu that would be completely unimaginable to them, strangers — as so many of us have once been — in a strange land.

Crisfield's note — and its arrival on the desk of then–Iowa Governor Robert Ray — is the third scene of this story. Ray responded to Crisfield's request, confident of what he has called "the generous spirit of the people of Iowa." Through his own efforts and with the full compliance of the federal government, Governor Ray welcomed the Tai Dam, as a people, to the Iowa prairies, to its cities and towns, to farmsteads on the gently rolling hills of its rich and yawning land. "As would be the case time and time again," Ray wrote recently, "Iowa organizations, churches, and individuals stepped forward to open their homes and their communities."

Strangers in a strange land

Scene four is best visualized in the Des Moines airport, where, on November 17, 1975, in three separate flights, three hundred Tai Dam refugees arrived from California.

That "homecoming" was not only the first, but also the most dramatic. All over the state, Iowans stood and waited at airports — in Sioux City, in Cedar Rapids, in Davenport — for Asian people the Iowa natives had never seen, a family or two, maybe more, maybe less. They waited to greet people who knew very little English or none at all, men, women, and children who would be bewildered at the fast pace of life in this vast nation of what seemed to them to be unimaginable wealth. All around the state, Iowans waited for people born and reared in a mountainous jungle landscape where there were no McDonald's, no little leagues, no apple pie or sweet corn, no spray-on furniture polish or vacuum cleaners — people who, in those first weeks of their arrival, needed assistance with food, shelter, clothing, and fuel in their every waking moment.

Much of the hard work of those first days had to be accomplished by volunteers, but the state government itself became involved in making life easier for the Tai Dam and other Southeast Asian refugees. Prior to their arrival, Governor Ray established the Governor's Task Force for Indochinese Resettlement, an employment service to hunt out jobs for the state's newest citizens.

Two years later, the scale of the effort was reduced as the flow of immigrants temporarily subsided. But in March of 1978, Governor Ray extended the program through September of 1981, in part because tens of thousands of Cambodian refugees had fled the killing fields to take up temporary residence in Thai refugee camps, from which they, too, needed relocation.

Less than a year later, Governor Ray watched a CBS documentary titled "The Boat People," and wrote a letter to then-President Carter, pledging to take 1,500 more Southeast Asian refugees in Iowa that year. Government agencies and commissions continued to ease the transition of the state's newest citizens in whatever ways they could, but the governor knew that government alone could not accomplish the assimilation necessary for vital community life. Real labors of love had to be undertaken and accomplished by volunteers and volunteer organizations.

Conflicts

Conflict in such a wide-scale, community adoption process inevitably arose. All across the state, as elsewhere in America, towns and communities were opening their arms, sometimes joyfully, sometimes not, to a wholly new tribe of residents. For reasons which are many, small agricultural communities — and Iowa is a network of small agricultural communities — are often the species of community most resistant to change — "this is the way we've always done it, after all." The image of small towns that some see in Grant Wood's *American Gothic* may well be a stereotype, but that doesn't mean its portrait isn't more than occasionally accurate. Most Iowans know that the local café, no matter how delightful its cinnamon rolls, can be, to strangers, an unwelcoming place. Already in September of 1979, with the refugee movement still in its early stages, a *Des Moines Register* poll found that more than half of the state's residents opposed the governor's resettlement campaigns.

But the governor was committed, on principle, to the notion that helping the people who had come to our aid in Southeast Asia demanded reciprocal action. It was, he maintained, the right thing to do.

The story we're telling begins in the broad outlines of world events, and it moves, with Governor Robert Ray's leadership, to a single, largely agricultural state in America's heartland. The questions created by the possibility of the influx of hundreds, even thousands, of new immigrants are not difficult to outline: "Bringing all those foreigners to our country—people who don't know a tractor from a combine—is that a good thing? My word, they can't even read a newspaper or fill out a tax form. And what about jobs? They're going to change our way of life—you can put your money on that."

As long as refugee resettlement was only an argument, opinions could be easily aired; the problem was theoretical. Soon enough, however, there were real people next door; in communities all over the state there were people who dressed strangely and cooked and ate bizarre foods. Throughout Iowa, some arms were open, some were crossed.

When houseguests cooked strange food in hot oil whose acrid fumes filled—and stayed—in every room, some people quickly turned up their noses. Some folks like their garlic in pinches; some in handfuls. Soon, what *smelled* turned into what *stank*.

"If you're going to live here, learn to eat decent," some thought—and said. "And if you want to be an American, learn English. You're here now—start acting like it." Anxiety soon turns defensive, and fear becomes bigotry.

Some became weary in well-doing, because in America investments must earn dividends. "If we break our backs to get what you need to get along in this town, you really ought to appreciate it—show some thanks. Show some gratitude."

What looked so gallant and noble could get downright difficult. "They want *what*? Do they think we're made of money? Give 'em a dime and they want a quarter; give 'em a buck and they want a five-spot. Ridiculous."

A volunteer I know from the first days of resettlement will never forget picking up a family from a local airport and bringing them that same night to a tiny basement apartment they'd worked hard to secure, showing them the nicely made beds they'd received when they asked around for donations. When these volunteers returned the next morning, they discovered—largely through hand gestures—what it was the town's newest residents wanted most. The woman rubbed her legs, pointing. They didn't understand. Then she rubbed her legs and pointed at theirs. Penniless, with no means of gaining a living at all, her cupboards still bare, standing on a real wood floor, not mud, for the first time in her life, this indigent refugee was telling them that, like nothing else, she wanted a pair of nylons.

A specific place

We've begun another chapter, another act, of this story. This chapter is set in one of hundreds of neighborhoods Governor Ray had imagined, a place where people took up his challenge to make refugees comfortable in a neighborhood that couldn't be more different from the *home* they would never forget on the other side of planet Earth.

In the state's far northwest corner, as elsewhere, the immigration process was ongoing by the late 1970s. Several churches in Sioux County sponsored refugee families, among them Bethel Christian Reformed of Sioux Center, Iowa, which very quickly took on sponsorship of several families, enlisting dozens of members to help.

Governor Robert Ray never knew Adrianna Dokter, although it's likely that she voted for him every time she could have when he ran for one of his five consecutive terms of office. What the governor was counting on in pledging the state's commitment to the flood of Asian refugees was a thousand Adrianna Dokters, men and women from around the state who would work tirelessly to help the newcomers find and then take a good strong hold of their own bootstraps.

Adrianna De Wit Dokter was born and reared on the kind of rural family farm that characterized the state's agriculture system in the early decades of the twentieth century, a mom-and-pop-and-kids operation with some hogs, some cattle, a few milk cows, and a bunch of pesky chickens. She was a Depression child, born in 1933, but like so many other rural kids her age, she likely never thought about the fact that times were tough during her childhood. Her parents were devout believers, sincere in their faith, given to having devotions at least three times a day—Scripture and prayer after every meal—people who wouldn't think of missing Sunday worship, attending twice each Sunday, in fact.

Adrianna became heir to a legacy of faith that frequently—and especially in her childhood home—placed devotion to God not only above any other human activity, but within every dimension of life. She came from a people easy to caricature as unflinchingly orthodox and emotionally dour, people lacking a sense of freedom and joy, God's "frozen chosen." Some of those types likely lived in her neighborhood and did, in fact, people the Dutch neighborhoods of Sioux County, Iowa. But she was not one of them, and neither were her parents.

> **Adrianna became heir to a legacy of faith that frequently—and especially in her childhood home—placed devotion to God not only above any other human activity, but within every dimension of life.**

Even today, forty percent of Sioux County children attend parochial or parental Christian schools, and so did the De Wit children, six of them in all, four sisters and two brothers—the Christian grade school in Hull and Western Christian High just down the block. Somewhere along the line, encouraged by a high school friend, Adrianna decided to be a teacher; when she graduated from high school she went on to college at nearby Northwestern, in Orange City.

A Bible teacher

From Northwestern, she took a teaching job in Rock Valley, at another Christian school, a combination class of fifth and sixth grades, with daily lesson plans that included a class called "Bible." As often happens, teachers become the best learners when they immerse themselves in their subject matter, and today, years later, Adrianna's sister Betty remembers that Adrianna's having to teach "Bible," especially the Old Testament, was its own kind of revelation for her. The kind of study that a teacher has to do made her an eager learner and even more a believer.

In 1953, Ed Dokter, from Sioux Center, a sometimes mechanic, sometimes hired man, all-around good guy, and (like Adrianna) a lover of classical music, came calling. Then, not long after, he left for the army, for Korea, at the very end of the Korean War. In Ed and Adrianna's case, absence did indeed make hearts grow fonder, their courtship not only maintained but encouraged by the good and heartfelt letters they exchanged. When he returned, they were married on June 27, 1956.

Aside from having graduated from college and taking a few trips to Michigan for some additional education, there's little to mark the life of Adrianna De Wit Dokter as different from any other young married woman of her era or area. Together, she and Ed raised three children, and she volunteered frequently, manning the polls for local and national elections, occasionally substituting in local schools, and working as an aide, sometimes teaching spelling and Bible or monitoring study halls.

Today, her children themselves describe their mother as fairly traditional back then—given to the kind of moral admonitions often characteristic of her people, the Dutch Reformed: wear dresses to church, not slacks; avoid showy-ness of any kind; keep up good Sabbath behavior; and, above all else, maintain a close relationship with the Lord. These were the major themes of their upbringing, they remember.

By 1982, when the refugees began to arrive, Adrianna Dokter was in a prime position to help. She'd been an educator, after all, and knew some things about teaching. With her youngest moving off to college, she found herself alone in a house that was much quieter than it had ever been and also much emptier. She may not have thought it at the time, but her children would say, today, knowing her, that she probably needed something to do. The ways of God are not always mysterious, after all.

Most important to her volunteering, they insist, was her personality, however. Her husband, Ed, quotes President Abraham Lincoln as a means by which to understand his wife's own character. "I don't like that fella," Lincoln once said, "I must seek to know him better."

What seems clear by the testimony of all who knew her is that Adrianna De Wit Dokter pulled up her nose at the small talk that is often the meat and potatoes of small-town life. She disliked the cliques that form too easily among people who see each other too regularly. She always was interested in current events and loved to discuss the pertinent political issues of the day. Above all, she was a believer who understood that faith made claims on her life that required her to be a steward of her time and pay attention to those in need. Adrianna De Wit Dokter may well have been exactly the kind of human being Governor Robert Ray imagined when he committed the entire state to helping the Asian people endangered by the sad end of the Vietnam War.

A child of war

There are many central characters in this story, but there is another we need to know up close and personal. In 1975, when Ed and Adrianna's kids were walking to the Christian school in town, Khay Baccam was on the other side of the world, still a teenager and already a master of the black market, dealing in scrap iron and contraband arms in Vientiane, Laos. Unlike many Asian refugees, Khay was not poor — he was rich, flipping out cold, hard cash to Laotian soldiers willing to sell their M-16s once the fighting stopped — and even when it hadn't. Maybe he was too young for political opinions; maybe he just didn't care. Whatever the case, Khay's great passion was money, the means by which to stay alive and achieve power. To politics and morality, he was, at best, indifferent.

Adrianna Dokter had grown up in a religious home on the plains of northwest Iowa, where her only experience of war was what she had heard about a world war many, many miles away, events probably out of the immediate consciousness of a child who hadn't, in the forties, yet come to what her church calls "the age of discretion."

Khay Baccam's father, however, a career soldier, had been a military commander on the wrong side of a war that had gone on for as long as his son could remember. As a child, Khay and his mother had willfully followed their father and husband wherever the battle lines took them. When finally his mother left her husband's side and went to Vientiane, Khay acquired his real education, not in a small-town Christian school, but on the messy streets of the capital city of a bloodied, war-torn country. On those streets' black markets, he made money.

It was the money—the amount he was known to control—that led thirty communist soldiers to surround his place one night. It was the money he threw around too publicly that got him into trouble. The new government simply assumed—incorrectly—that this big-time operator had to be an American collaborator, an enemy of the people.

Not long after his arrest, he found himself in a prison compound in northern Laos, a camp so remote that there was no need for walls or fences. There, for three long months, his feet and hands were bound by wire so tight that he could not walk to get food or use the latrine. In that time, his wrists turned gray, limp, and lifeless, his forearms swelled like sausages. Hope fled. All that remained in him was instinct, the stubborn will to survive.

While Ed and Adrianna were going to their kids' high school basketball games, Khay Baccam, his hands finally freed, was still in prison, drawing pictures on the blades of his captors' swords, slowly gaining thereby some respect. Cars and motorcycles on the backs of T-shirts and military uniforms, tattoos in all varieties and colors—his drawings kept him alive.

In northwest Iowa, while Ed and Adrianna were doing daily devotions with their children after supper, Khay Baccam remained a prisoner in the camp at Ou Tai, Laos, where one night a guard came in lugging a bag the prisoners thought held cigarettes. When the guard reached in, he pulled out the mutilated head of someone who had tried to escape, a moral lesson of a different kind.

Eventually, the government simply abandoned the prison at Ou Tai because it was of no more use, and Khay Baccam joined 150 starving ex-prisoners on a long walk back to Vientiane, each of them carrying nothing more than blankets, their backs covered with their only suit of ragged clothes.

When finally they arrived, the city was under attack from the air. People shouted at them to run and hide or be killed. "We've come back from the dead," Khay told them. "We are beyond the grip of death."

In 1981, at just about the time that Ed and Adrianna had moved their church membership to a new fellowship because their home church, Bethel Christian Reformed, had simply become too large, Khay Baccam sat in a shallow pond of water and watched the Thai refugee camp where he lived go up in smoke and flames. Many people died that night, but he and others, including his new wife, Feuang, took refuge in the fish ponds on the perimeter of the camp to avoid the flames and searing heat.

A memorable example

The next day, the refugees witnessed something they'd never seen before — Christian people, Roman Catholic sisters, dispensing aid and comfort, food and clothing and blankets, to the dispossessed. Strangely, at least to him, those women asked nothing, required nothing, in return. He'd always believed — as did others — that the Roman Catholics were not to be trusted because their priests required Laotian men to sacrifice their wives' sexual favors in exchange for marrying a couple. But these Roman Catholics, these Christians, required nothing, simply gave, offered real help to the suffering people, many of whom were burned in the fire.

Khay pointed at them and spoke to his mother-in-law.

"You see what they do?" he asked. "The Christians come to help. Did you ever give them anything before? No—but they give everything to us."

One night, again a world away, at one of the first meetings of the Evangelism Committee of the newly established Faith Christian Reformed Church, Sioux Center, a man who had worked with Asian refugees in the area from the beginning, Dr. Al Mennega, a professor of biology at Dordt College, asked if that committee would take it upon themselves to provide the means by which a new Laotian family could resettle in Sioux Center. The Baccams—this new family—were the son and daughter-in-law of a couple already there, he said, and their names were Khay and Feuang. And they had a baby, a little girl named Soudalay. They need sponsorship, he told them.

It was something they could do, they thought, something they should do. They said yes.

Congregational life was just beginning at Faith Christian Reformed Church, and Mennega's proposal looked like the kind of project that made sense to a brand new committee. Refugee sponsorship wasn't totally new—Bethel and other churches had already been working with a number of families. It was something they could do, they thought, something they should do. They said yes.

Back in the Thai refugee camp, the man called "the captain," the chair of the refugee board, looked down at the papers in his hands and then up again at the young man and his wife and baby standing before him. Even though he had been a resident of that camp, Khay Baccam had run military secrets—and other things—back and forth for months across national borders, providing a service the captain understood. In many ways, the captain didn't want Khay Baccam to leave because he was performing a dangerous but valuable service.

But Khay had made up his mind. After being injured in a motorcycle accident, he had seen his new wife in a different light, not simply an accessory but a partner, someone who loved him and was willing, in ways he wasn't, to serve him. He'd begun to realize that his life of intrigue and danger, as full of excitement as it was, had not been healthy for his new relationship. In some ways, the thought of being more domestic seemed almost more perilous to him than the dangers that threatened him on his secret trips back and forth across the Thai border. But a voice within him made it clear that this difficult path, the one that led to his being more of a husband, more of a servant, was the one he should take, not the other, not the old way. And that new way of life would be easier in a new world.

The captain shrugged his shoulders and looked down once again at the papers before him. "Faith Christian Church," he said. "A church for a sponsor is a good thing." He sat back behind his desk and tapped the papers with his pencil. "A church will do much to help you."

Not long after Dr. Mennega's visit to that evangelism committee, one of the members called Adrianna Dokter. Adrianna had been a teacher, after all, and a spelling and language teacher—and the committee needed someone to tutor this new family, to try to introduce them to the lingual currency of this new country. Would Adrianna think about doing it?

She said yes.

Lessons in language

And thus begins chapter four, act four, of our story, a chapter that appears to end, sadly, with something as entirely unforeseen as had been the meeting of such vastly different people in the heart of farm country, a small town at the western edge of a state known principally for corn and soybeans, hogs and cattle, thousands of miles from mountainous Asian jungles.

On the night of August 5, 2002, twenty years after she'd begun what she was asked to do with Khay and Feuang Baccam, that is, teach them the English language, Adrianna

De Wit Dokter came home, sat down in the rocker, and had a stroke that, two days later, ended her life.

In terms of this earth, her sudden and untimely death ended a dear and tender relationship that had grown into something far more than teacher and students, a relationship all of them treasured.

How did that happen? There's the mystery, an eternal mystery.

But there are things we know. Adrianna's husband and her children are convinced that their mother changed as a result of her weekly lessons and her often daily communication with Khay and Feuang. When she'd talk to her sister Betty in private—something she often did just because she needed to—she'd tell her that something she hadn't entirely foreseen was happening in this man, this ex-black marketer, this former concentration camp refugee, and it was something that astounded her. "He sees the big picture," she used to say to Betty—and to others. "I just know that he sees the big picture."

But so did she, according to her family. This young Asian man and his wife, so different from the rest of the Dokter's neighbors, taught them—Adrianna first, and then Ed, too—that there was a bigger picture than the immediate concerns of church and school and family. Not that those interests were somehow wrong or misguided, but Adrianna De Wit Dokter began to understand that the Christian life has far broader concerns than Sabbath observance or its own limited sense of orthodoxy.

Calvinist that she was, Adrianna Dokter would not want anyone to say that she "brought Khay Baccam to the Lord," as some believers might be fond of saying. An old-line believer in God's sovereignty, she would, her family says, be far more comfortable with a description of what happened between them stated this way: God brought Khay—and Feuang—home to his love; Adrianna was only an agent, an instrument, and not even the only one.

You may call that difference "semantic" if you want to,

but Adrianna would call it, with all seriousness, theology. A line penciled onto her notes for a speech to volunteers helping other Asian refugees says this: "One man cannot do ministry; many men cannot do ministry. Only God can change hearts."

And there is more to Khay's eventual conversion to Christianity than two decades of long and devoted conversations over the coffee Adrianna loved to share; there's more than the language training that became so much broader than mere words. There is, after all, that memory of gracious nuns giving selflessly, expecting nothing in return, a transaction so incredible that it stopped him in his tracks. Khay Baccam had never been much of a believer in anything, but Adrianna Dokter was not his Savior — and he knows that, too. His salvation belongs to the Lord.

Today, Khay Baccam is a preacher, an evangelist, a Bible study leader, a mentor to dozens, even hundreds of Lao and Tai Dam people in a region that spreads from Sioux City, Iowa, north to the Twin Cities of Minnesota, west to South Dakota, and sometimes as far east as Des Moines. To God be the glory, forever and ever, Adrianna would say. But we'll violate no doctrine of Calvinist theology if we maintain, as humbly as she would, that she was, through those precious years, a blessed instrument of God's peace.

What happened?

This chapter of the story requires a bit more, however. As Governor Ray himself knows, not all refugee stories end as triumphantly as this one appears to. Sometimes sponsors felt conned by families who took greedily from the heartfelt offerings of an entire community and then, at times even without notice, simply left, as though those gifts were nothing at all. Not all language tutoring ended in graduations. But then, not all gifts were heartfelt either; occasionally, people used the refugees as a receptacle for the junk they cleared from their basements.

Why did this particular relationship flourish as it did? What *exactly* happened here?

If there were tapes of every meeting of Adrianna Dokter and Khay Baccam, might we be able to find the exact moment when the roles assigned became something else altogether? When "teacher" and "student" took on new meanings? Because there was a "crossing over" here, an exchange of roles: the teacher became student, the student became teacher. All of her children know it and will tell you as much—"Mom learned so much from Khay"—while he undoubtedly learned so much from her. They became equals in this blessed human transaction; they nurtured each other, strengthened each other, changed each other.

At her funeral, Khay told a story that comes close to answering the question of how what happened between them, did.

He told the family and friends that he'd come to this country in 1982. "I am Asian, Laotian," he said, and never once did anyone ask him what he believed or whether he'd fit into the community. "I never heard one such word," he told them. He held up a Bible, the Bible he'd received from her long ago, an old one scarred by a circle where a hundred cups of coffee had left their mark. "This shows how much she liked to drink coffee," he said.

> **Because there was a "crossing over" here, an exchange of roles: the teacher became student, the student became teacher. . . . They nurtured each other, strengthened each other, changed each other.**

When he'd go to church to fulfill the expectations of his sponsors, to respect the commitment that they were giving him and his family, he said that he remembered noticing that only some people would talk to him—Adrianna was one of them, this same Adrianna who was, every Wednesday, coming to his house to teach him the English language.

For almost two years, those teaching sessions continued,

every week on Wednesday. One day, he said, he asked her a question that had been weighing on him. "Adrianna," he said, "why do you come over here? — you don't have other work? You just sit here and listen to me talk, talk, talk," he told her. "But I want to hear something from you."

Adrianna told him, he said, that she was afraid he wouldn't understand what it was she wanted him to hear.

"Just tell me," he told her. "Don't be afraid of making mistakes — just tell me."

She told him that she'd been waiting for a long time for him to ask what he did — "many months and days" — and that now she could tell him what she felt, and then she said it: "I love you — I love your family. I am here and I am teaching you and I want you to know the Lord Jesus Christ."

Khay told the mourners at Adrianna's funeral that he sat there for a moment and did nothing, then saw something that he'd never forget — tears. He told himself he was nothing but an ordinary Laotian man so why would she cry for him? "What is it about *me* that is so important?" he asked himself. And then he looked at himself, he said, and cried, too.

"Something happened," he told the people in Faith Church, and he looked at the Bible with the coffee-cup circle. "Something is in that book," and that's what he told Adrianna right then and there. "I would like to know more about that — what is in that book. Tell me more about that, too."

For the next twenty years, Adrianna Dokter was his teacher; but that morning, the morning when he asked her what it was that made her the Adrianna he'd come to respect and love, that morning he became more than just a student and she became far more than a teacher. Something heartfelt, something transcending language, passed between them.

When he began his story, Khay explained how thankful he was for the opportunity to say a few words, for "giving me a chance to speak about my friend . . ." Then he stopped, paused for just a moment, searching for just the right words, " — and I would say," he told them, "my *mom*, too, because when I speak she understands."

A story without end

What exactly Governor Robert Ray wanted to occur in the state of Iowa when he asked people to welcome Southeast Asian refugees is a question only Governor Ray himself can answer. But what we can say with confidence is that a significant part of what happened between Adrianna Dokter and Khay Baccam is somewhere at the heart of his vision, because commitment and service created real and lasting friendship and more — love.

Christian believers will maintain that the most significant story in the relationship between Adrianna De Wit Dokter and Khay Baccam is how Khay himself, someone who knew nothing about the Christian faith, not only came to believe in Jesus Christ, but also began to spread the good news of salvation to others, his friends and his people. That eternal story is the music most people will be singing when they finish the story.

But there is another story here too, and it is just as eternal, just as life-changing, because Khay Baccam, as much an instrument of God's eternal will and counsel as Adrianna herself, deeply affected and even changed the life of Adrianna Dokter. "If you always do what you've always done," she scribbled into her notes for a speech preparing volunteers to work with Asian refugees, "you'll always get what you've always got."

On the very day she suffered a stroke, Adrianna wrote an e-mail note to the first pastor of Faith Church, Rev. Dave Smit, who was, at that time, residing in California. In that note, she told him how plans for the new vacation Bible school at Sioux City's Lao Unity Church were progressing and how aware she was — even after twenty years — of the differences that exist between the two cultures, specifically in planning and carrying out plans. "Oh well," she wrote, "it doesn't hurt us to bend a bit . . . . Maybe God put the Laotians in our path so we would see the broader picture of the gospel."

If there's one thing that Adrianna herself would want us to remember about all of this—if she could return right now and ramble on about the last twenty years of her relationships with the Lao community in northwest Iowa—it's likely she would tell us that *she* was the recipient of grace, that the joy was hers, that the blessings of those years are, as the old song claims, "all mine, and ten thousand beside."

And that is something that all of us—those who ascribe to the Christian faith and those who do not—can agree upon. Even though it always asks a great deal of us, selfless love replenishes far more than it requires.

There is no end to this story—no end but eternity. It resides, like all our stories, and like the ones that follow, in the whole counsel of the Lord our God.

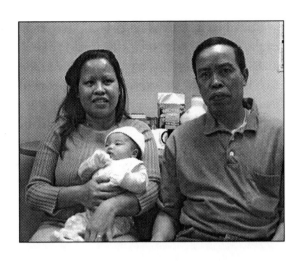

SAWAN AND
HONGTHONG SIRI

....

Smiling Faces, Answered Prayers

Americans of European descent sometimes find the polite grins of many Asian people more than a bit disconcerting because they don't know how to read all of those smiles, nor the people who wear them. Sociologists have offered theories as to why so many Asians frequently wear such joyful public faces, but the fact remains — lots of European-Americans, accustomed to a good deal less civility, find such well-mannered behavior baffling.

Hongthong Siri wears just such a smile when you meet her, whether or not she is toting along her newborn, Abbey, born January 9, 2005. But in this case, if you know at least something of her story, it's not hard to explain why this young woman, so new to North America, should be joyous. She has, after all, a new, healthy baby girl, her first child. She should be happy.

But if you know more of her story, the joy beneath the smile is even more understandable. Immense changes have occurred in her life in the last year, so many that it's almost impossible not to wonder whether really all is well within her life – and her soul.

There's Abbey, after all – and Abbey is fine, healthy, and growing. But there's also this: a year ago, Hongthong was working in a textile factory just outside of Vientiane, Laos. She was without a spouse, a high school graduate – and she wasn't necessarily on the lookout for a husband or a child or a life in a new country.

But along came Sawan Siri, a man who was, not long ago, completely unknown to her and her family, a man from a world unimaginably far away, a friend of a friend's friend – well, that's not totally accurate, so let's try it again: Sawan Siri, the man who today is her husband and the father of her baby, was, not all that long ago, a friend of a friend's boyfriend.

One day at the factory, that friend told her about this boyfriend she had in the United States, a man who was likely to become more than just a boyfriend. "And by the way," she said, "he has a friend, too, a friend who is not married."

Now Lao women, by custom, are not aggressive; neither she nor her friend could simply advance the notion that Hongthong might well hook up with this American friend-of-a-boyfriend. But the message – the opportunity to consider possibilities – was communicated from Vientiane all the way back to Worthington, Minnesota, where Sawan Siri was living and working.

"A big, big problem in my life"

By his own description, Sawan was single and lonely. He'd been married for seventeen years to a woman who left him, in 1999, for another man. He says he knew that things weren't going well in his marriage, but what happened surprised him nonetheless and just about broke his heart. He and his wife had been together ever since the refugee camp at Napho, Thailand; in fact, she was originally from the small Laotian village he'd once called home, Banken, in Baklai, northern Laos.

Together, they had three children, the oldest two born already in Thailand. Together, they'd been living in Worthington, Minnesota, for nine years, since 1990. What happened to them — between them — was devastating. "It was," he says, with understatement, "a big, big problem in my life."

Now this friend of Sawan's, this man with the girlfriend in the Vientiane textile factory, made the long trip to Laos to confirm his relationship. And that's where the word got out — she had a good friend back in the factory, someone who just might make a match for this Laotian man in America named Sawan.

Correspondence began between them, slowly, tentatively, then, eventually, with a touch more earnestness. Soon enough, their letters warmed, and possibilities for this relationship began to emerge more clearly in Sawan's mind — and Hongthong's.

Sawan determined to make a trip back to Laos because he wanted to meet this woman, this friend of a friend. He was, back then — as he is today — a believer in Jesus Christ. His divorce from his first wife had taught him that faith in Jesus doesn't necessarily mean an end to sadness. But even though his heart had been broken, he never stopped praying, never stopped asking the Lord for peace and resolution.

So all during the flight and then again on the runway when they touched down in Vientiane, Sawan says he and his friend were in constant prayer about this trip, about this meeting, about these women, both of them. "Before I went to Laos," he says, "I prayed to God — every time I go to sleep or eat. I had a broken heart, and I didn't want to have another one."

He knew that moving forward into another relationship had its own unseen risks. Love, sometimes, doesn't conquer all. He didn't know this woman named Hongthong, not really. Along with his letters, he'd been sending her tracts, Christian tracts, to read and study so she would know who he was — a Christian. He knew very well that all of this letter-writing could end, once again, with a kind of pain similar to the one he hadn't really put totally behind him.

"But I told myself I was still young," he says when he remembers. "And I told myself I didn't want to be single for the rest of my life. I would like to have someone to share my life."

He'd already talked to his oldest child, his daughter, and asked her if she thought that he could see another woman, someone other than her mother. He says she wasn't terribly pleased at the prospect, and her tentative reaction contributed to his fear as he sat, in prayer, on the runway in Vientiane, just before stepping off the plane.

"Lord," he said, "I pray to you to help me know if she will become my future wife — if it's your will. I don't want to be hurt again." There in the seat, he prayed, they both did, the plane idling up to the gate. The whole event seemed to have very high stakes.

And then something happened that makes him smile, makes him laugh, in fact, to remember it — makes Hongthong laugh, too, because what occurred seemed so divinely planned. When he and his friend descended from that plane, those two women were standing right there. He says that neither he nor his friend expected that, and when he saw Hongthong waiting — the first time he'd ever laid eyes on her — and when that happened so quickly after they'd ended their very earnest prayers, it was as though the Lord God Almighty had engineered an answer to their supplications. The story wasn't over, but Hongthong seemed, in so many ways, to be an antidote to his heartache and loneliness and, even more, a veritable answer to prayer.

There in the seat, he prayed, they both did, the plane idling up to the gate.

Soon they were engaged, and he made the trek to her village to begin the process by which they could be married. That process, given U.S. immigration laws, takes several months — seven in this case, from the time Sawan left Laos at the end of that visit, until he could return to bring Hongthong to Worthington to be his wife. But by the time he left, he was confident that this woman was someone he wanted to see again—and again.

More prayers

During those seven months, there was more correspondence, more tracts, more phone calls. When he returned, he was confident that all of his papers—and there were many—were in order. He hoped—and once again he prayed, fervently—that everything would work according to what he'd come to believe was God's own plan for his life.

But this time the prayers were different, he says. This time, "there were many more thank-yous to the Lord," he remembers. But there was also supplication: prayers for safety on the trip and prayers for the interview with American customs. Hongthong needed to be interviewed so that customs officials would be sure she wasn't fabricating a story simply to immigrate. If she failed that interview, the whole lengthy process would have to begin again, something neither of them wanted.

Picture it this way—Hongthong facing a grilling from the American immigration officials, Sawan praying constantly. The customs people wanted to know the story, the whole story—who was this man named Sawan Siri? What were the names of his children? Where did he live in the United States? That she could answer those specific questions correctly and without hesitation determined her—and their—fate. She had to demonstrate that this marriage wasn't something thrown together willy-nilly.

Hongthong passed, easily. Prayers were being answered. Things were looking good.

On the other hand, Sawan, a committed Christian, someone who had been growing in the Lord for almost twenty years, found himself estranged from his own people when they insisted on a Laotian celebration that included the spirit worship he was committed not to practice. He had become a Christian believer, he told the people who'd gathered to party with him; there were things he wouldn't do. Not all of them understood.

Hongthong returned to the States with him in August, and they were married soon after by Pastor Sone Dedthanou in the Lao Church of Worthington.

So several months later, when Sawan and Hongthong Siri stood in front of the people in that same Laotian church and had their daughter baptized, Hongthong, who'd lived in this country for less than a year, had reason to smile. Much had changed, and much had changed very quickly in her life. In a matter of a year, she'd become a wife, she'd become a mother, and she'd become an American. Furthermore, she was—and is—becoming a believer.

With less than a year in this country, is she sometimes lonely for the life she left behind in Laos? "Sad, sometimes," she says, being away from her family for the first time and so terribly far away, too. But it is bearable, she claims, because she can, so often, talk to them on the phone. "They ask me, 'Is everything okay?' and I tell them, 'Yes.'"

He was, by Christian standards, a believer in many spirits and many gods.

Her husband, who prayed so hard that Hongthong would be the wife he wanted and needed, is a fine man, in part, she'd say, because he is a Christian and, therefore, is not a gambler or a drunk. He doesn't smoke—tobacco or anything else. He is neither an abuser nor a philanderer. He is a Christian. That's the way he might say it himself.

But of course, he wasn't always a believer in Jesus Christ, the Son of God. He was raised, as were so many of his friends, within a specific faith tradition and by way of occasional religious practice; in his case, that faith was vague and mysterious, a hybrid spirituality composed of equal parts Buddhism and spirit worship. He was, by Christian standards, a believer in many spirits and many gods.

His story, however, is as unique as each of us is, under heaven. For some Lao people, Christianity begins to appear as an alternative when they have nowhere else to go, their own lives in shambles. For some, the gifts of good Christian people create a testimony that makes them want to know more; when they seek truth, they find it in the revealed Word of God, in preaching, in Bible studies. Others find their way by associating with Christian friends whose lives are themselves testimonies to strength and conviction. For most Lao people, and for all of us, coming to Christ is often a pilgrimage of some considerable length.

But Sawan Siri says he became a believer in Jesus Christ very soon after the very first time he attended Christian worship. It was 1981, and his cousin, Vieng, invited him to go to church with her in the camp at Soptuant. "Today is Sunday," she told him. "You want to go to church with me?"

He said yes, and from then on, he attended every Sunday while they lived in that camp.

But his claiming Jesus as Savior required more than a single visit to Christian worship. He says he'd been haunted by his fear of the spirit world and was even afraid of the dark. Those fears tormented him and didn't miraculously stop that first Sunday.

After a short time, Vieng told him that he lacked true faith if he was still afraid of spirits. "You don't believe with your whole heart," she told him. "If you put all your fears into your faith in the Lord Jesus Christ, then, after that, you will fear the spirits no more."

Sunday after Sunday, he went to church. Day after day, he prayed. Day after day, he tried to study the Holy Scriptures. Finally, the assurance that Vieng claimed was given to those who truly believe became his. "Now I have no fear, no more," he told his cousin. And from that day, Sawan marks his conversion, even though he will readily admit that he had so much more to learn. He didn't understand, nor did he really know much at all about what had occurred in his heart. What was undeniable, however, was that his fears, which had so frequently haunted him, had simply vanished. That was all it took for him to know that there was something eternally true about this new Christian faith.

From that point on, he says, he was a believer. He'd started by attending a small church in the camp, with maybe a dozen people. But soon he and Vieng and others went into the nearby Thai village and worshiped with many others at a church where he was baptized as one of God's own children in 1981.

Since that time, Sawan will be happy to tell you that he's grown in the faith. But what's unusual about his story is the miracle of such a full and almost immediate reception of the truth of the Christian story.

The camp at Soptuant

But there is more to Sawan's story that makes it unique. Unlike so many other Laotian people who've immigrated, Sawan's father was *not* a soldier and had *not* fought the communist regime. His father was in no trouble with authorities, but his father urged his son, Sawan, as well as his older brother, to cross the border because the authorities were looking to draft young men into the military. The only way to avoid conscription, his father told him, was to escape to Thailand.

There are no concentration camps in Sawan's story. He went to Thailand, to a refugee camp, to escape a draft, yes — but he also went to find a better life.

And the camp at Soptuant, province of Nan, Thailand, was not a particularly evil place. Unlike so many other Laotian refugees, Sawan Siri didn't suffer horrifying deprivation. In fact, the refugees there were allowed to leave the confines of the place to find odd jobs outside the camp. Soptuant wasn't a nightmarish prison, really.

And there's more. Sawan Siri was not obsessed by the dream of escaping his homeland or the camp itself. Life wasn't all that bad, he says. Both at Soptuant and the subsequent camp where he lived, Sinh Kham, he was a teacher who, under supervision of the United Nations, taught Laotian children and teenagers their own Lao language. Teaching was a good job and paid well. He had some prestige, in fact, enough so that, when coming to the second camp, a few of his former students from Soptuant recognized him and asked him to teach them again. Things were never really desperate for Sawan Siri.

His only excursion into danger, into war, seems now, to him, almost silly. In Soptuant, a friend enlisted him and others to sneak back to Laos and fight the communist regime. When he remembers his short time as a revolutionary, he can't hold back his laughter. For some time, he and others trained, then finally crossed the border, ready to go to battle, scraping for a fight. But once the communists discovered what was going on, they sent an army to repel the ragamuffin rebels, who had no weaponry to speak of. The memories return in waves of laughter. A few rounds from enemy guns, his only glimpse of combat, and the whole bunch high-tailed it back to Thailand.

When a cousin who'd already gone to America acted as his sponsor, he and his first wife, along with their two children, finally immigrated and found a home in Sioux City, Iowa, where they both got jobs at Iowa Beef Processors. Life was good, but the family had troubles because both husband and wife worked the same shift, making the kids—and soon there were three—a difficult burden. A year later, in 1990, they moved to Worthington, when a cousin told him Swift Packing offered separate daytime shifts. Family responsibilities would be easier to manage.

Nine years later, his wife left. There was another man, finally, but for a longer time there was also another faith. Her father, who'd also immigrated, was an important figure in the old religion, spirit worship. Occasionally, Sawan would accompany his wife to attend spirit worship, the rites. But the more he studied the Bible, he says, the more he learned about this Christian God and the less he felt at home in the old ways.

His wife never attended Christian worship with him, he says, and their relationship fell into silence, then shattered when she found another man.

For three years he was alone and very sad. He says that he passed by opportunities when other women told him they would gladly give him a child, but by this time, he was a believer who wouldn't have any part of what was being offered.

That's when he started to write this friend of a friend's friend back in Vientiane. And soon, after those first few exchanged letters, he started praying for this woman, Hongthong, and for himself, for wisdom and patience and love.

Early in that exchange, she told him that she would like to come to the United States, but she had to be sure that he was a good person. "You can be my husband," she told him, "if I know you can take care of my family well."

He told her he had a good job—quality control at Swift, made a good wage. He would be a handsome provider.

And when they met—when she and her friend stood just off the runway at the airport in Vientiane and met them as they descended the stairs, she says that she could see in his heart that he was what he said he was—a good person. All of this, Sawan insists, was an answer to prayer. Who can doubt him?

Sawan Siri will never forget how, early in his Christian life, a pastor opened the Word to John 3:16, telling him and all who gathered in that small church in the camp that the promise of the gospel was that all who believed in Jesus Christ would be saved, would be kept safe forever, eternally, would not be punished.

Not punished.

"Do you know what *punished* means?" he says that preacher asked them. "It means your life is ended."

That sermon he's never forgotten, he says, because right then and there he told himself that he didn't want his life to end. "The only way not to lose your life is to believe in the Lord Jesus Christ," that preacher said.

He didn't want to lose his life. "Then what must I do? Believe in him?"

And the preacher said, yes, you have to believe.

Something about that sermon made him believe. There was no way he would pull away from the Lord, he says, because he didn't want to lose that life. He wanted no part of an end. He wanted life. He chose to live and live eternally.

"Life is very beautiful," he told himself then — and says yet today. "Life is very beautiful — I know that."

And that's why you see him smile, unforgettably — a smile, by the way, that's catching.

KEO AND BOONJUN PHOMMARATH

No, Never Alone

Painted with the broadest strokes possible, Keo Phomma-rath's story creates a circle — he left home as a child, very much alone, and then returned, twenty-six years later, a wholly different man.

His is the story of a child left behind in a corner of the world he knew nothing about, but a child who finally returns, phenomenally, years later. In no sense is the story of Keo Phommarath the story of a prodigal son, even though wine, women, and song became the triumphs of his youth. He never departed from his mother's faith, not until much later, just before he returned to Laos as a new man in Jesus. That radical change makes his homecoming even more remarkable.

What Keo Phommarath saw, almost every day as a boy, was a line of believers coming to his house, one after another, to speak and pray with his father, a practitioner of ancient spiritism. If you need safety in battle, see Mr. Phommarath, who will give you just a few words on a small piece of paper and ask you to bind it to your chest in times of great danger. He says that he will pray unceasingly for you to come out of the war alive. You want to speak to a woman about love but don't have the right words? Not to worry. Mr. Phommarath will give you something to smooth on your lips and you'll have the eloquence of a poet.

From miles around they came, because Keo's father could turn one's life around with little more than a shred of paper, a pinch of ointment, and a soothing promise.

But Keo's father had no interest in passing along his spiritism to Keo, his second son. His father sensed, Keo says, a different spirit in him, a spirit closer to his wife's Buddhism. For that reason, Keo never learned his father's way. Instead, he entered the temple. His head was shaved, his body enrobed, and, still a child, he spent four years training to be the monk his mother wanted him to be, a monk like his beloved grandfather.

When he remembers those days now, he laughs a bit, because he thinks of his grandfather, the monk, as being a bit more selfish than devout, more interested in having his grandson around to rub his feet and wash his clothes than concerned about the boy's religious upbringing. Nonetheless, Keo stayed in the temple, read the Buddhist scriptures, learned the commandments, and became, in a way, a disciple.

And although he left the temple at age thirteen, Keo Phommarath will tell you that, for most of his life, he remained the Buddhist his mother wanted him to be. Thirty years later, leading a praise band in a Christian church in faraway North America, the ornaments of his Buddhist faith still hung around his neck as he sang about this Jesus. "I was still a Buddhist," he'll tell you today. "I always was a Buddhist."

It was to Buddha he prayed when he crossed the Mekong River to Thailand, alone. His father wanted his two oldest boys to live, not die as mercenaries for the communist insurgency, who were recruiting—conscripting, really.

His mother didn't want her boys to leave, of course; she was terrified that she'd never see her two oldest children again. She cried, cried hard, he remembers, but his father claimed that there was no other way. He believed that staying at home meant death; he wanted them safe across the river in Thailand.

Crossing over

And so, in 1975, two Phommarath boys began a dangerous journey from Penpao, through jungles and strange villages, doing what they could to avoid the communist soldiers. For three days they walked, often crawling along on their bellies to avoid being seen.

Around them, they knew that there was killing. They heard people screaming, dying. Bullets flew past them into the jungle. "I knew what was happening," he says, "and I was very scared."

When, in the middle of the night, they finally arrived at the Mekong River, they met with others who wanted to escape. Friendly forces helped them locate a navigable spot out of the line of fire of the communists, but there were too many to go across the river in one boat. The children were sent first.

That's when his brother told him, shockingly, that he was going to stay and join the opposition forces. "You go on," he told Keo.

Keo had no idea where he was going.

"I am going to stay here," his brother told him. He pointed at the others who were leaving. "They will find a safe place for you."

He remembers his own tears at that moment, and he will never forget the near silence of the paddles through the river as the flimsy little boat made its way toward the other side.

His heart was racing. Gunfire could erupt at any moment and blow them out of the water. "If they saw you, that was it," he says, pointing his finger like a rifle. He was a boy, only thirteen. "I didn't know a thing," he says. "I didn't even know what a camp was, and I tell you what — I didn't like it, not at all."

But at least he was safe. When he first arrived at the refugee camp, he lived with the family of one of the men who had helped the refugees cross the Mekong River. What followed, shortly after, was a month in jail, a kind of holding tank for Laotian refugees, a place where many Laotians were kept until their identification could be documented, a dangerous place where fighting broke out constantly. One man — Keo doesn't even remember his name — protected him, almost like the father he'd left behind in Penpao, until, finally, he was returned to the refugee camp. More than a few of his memories are not good.

He remembers his own tears at that moment, and he will never forget the near silence of the paddles through the river as the flimsy little boat made its way toward the other side.

There was no going back, of course. If Keo Phommarath was going to make his way through the mess before him — and, seemingly, through life itself — it would be on his own, by way of his own initiative, his spunk, his instincts.

He didn't care much for life in the camps, he says, so when a Thai family asked him if he'd be interested in working with them on their farm, he left.

The word *immigration* was not in his vocabulary at the time. He was little more than a boy and had very little sense of his own future. He wanted only to stay alive, and what he knew more than anything was that he missed his family. "I missed my mom," he remembers. "I missed my dad. I missed my family. I never thought about America."

For the next two years, he worked for that family, who eventually came to adopt him, in a way, and to trust him. He lived away from the household the last year, working in the family's upholstery shop. Though not yet sixteen, in his words, he "did it all." The parties, the girls, the booze, the drugs — all of that delighted him enough to help him forget home. "Drugs, drinking, gangs, you know? —I thought it was cool."

When the upholstery business went bankrupt because of his excesses, his Thai family was very angry, he says. The woman who'd given him so much love turned on him. "You're bad," she screamed. "You're a refugee from nowhere, and you're bad. I gave you so much and look at what you've done to me."

Once more, he was alone. Keo Phommarath couldn't go home, back to Laos. The only place he could go was to the refugee camp he'd left, and that's when he decided, for the first time, that he needed something better, some new place, a new opportunity. He began to think about leaving Thailand.

When word came to Laos that Keo was back in the Thai refugee camp, his mother sent him a message to meet her at the Mekong River because she wanted badly to see him, to speak to him.

He received permission to leave, and he met her for the first time in several years. She cried, he says. They both did, and then she begged him, please, to come home. He was, after all, her child, she told him. What Keo couldn't forget, however, was his father's warning about being dragged into the communist army. What's more, in the camp he'd found a girlfriend and moved in with her. He loved her. Even though he also loved his mother dearly, he honestly didn't want to go back.

"If you don't come with me," she said, "right now I will jump into the river."

There they stood in the darkness, the roiling water beneath them. Not for one moment did he doubt her promise. "What could I do? I didn't want her to die," he says. "I love my mother."

Penpoa, once more

For three weeks, he stayed in the village of Penpoa, his brothers and sisters happy to have him back, even though some of them barely remembered him, nor he them. But he'd lived too long on his own, and it was difficult for him to live, once more, under the authority of his parents, even though he loved them.

News from the camp reached him in Penpoa that his name had climbed to the top of the list of those eligible to leave for America. What's more, he wanted no part of being drawn into the army, and he still had this girlfriend he loved, someone who knew nothing of what had happened to him the night he went to see his mother.

So when he left his parents' home, he sneaked away, even stole money from his parents' pockets, then ran off, headed back across the river.

This time he was alone. He took off all his clothes, packed them in a plastic bag he tied to his leg, grabbed a bamboo shoot in case he needed to breathe from beneath the surface, and headed across. He heard the communists, then prayed hard for his escape. When he made it to the other side, unseen, he was so exhausted that he fell asleep on the bank.

He was only seventeen years old.

A month later, he got on a plane and flew to America. Because they were not married, his girlfriend could not go with him. That was a very sad time, he remembers, because she ran alongside the bus as he left, tears in her eyes.

Once more, Keo Phommarath was all alone. This time, when he looked around, he found himself on a new continent. "I don't know anybody," he says, laughing today, so many years later. "I don't know anybody in all of this country," he remembers. If he was going to make it here, once again he was going to have to use his own ingenuity.

For the first few weeks in a hotel in Washington D.C., all he ate was noodles. "I didn't like it at the hotel," he says. "It wasn't my food — not my sticky rice. Everything is bread, and I miss my mom, I miss Thailand, and there's nothing I can do, nowhere to run. In Laos, I could at least run around some, but not here."

Disoriented, he turned to other refugees around him. "I talked to the others, but no one understood anything, you know? 'I'm lost, too,' they'd say. 'You're asking me how to get along here? — I'm lost myself.' Everybody was lost."

His sponsors wanted him to take English language training, and he did, several afternoons a week, but he was less interested in language than he was in freedom, and something told him that the means to freedom was money. He wanted a job. He didn't want to be stuck in school, didn't want to be educated.

He wanted freedom, and he told his sponsors as much, so they got him a job in a sprawling chicken farm factory in Maryland City, Maryland. Money began to roll in, but life was unsettled and difficult because the other workers weren't Lao people, but Chinese, Cambodians, Vietnamese, all of them with their own languages. The factory was a confusion of tongues and people.

Several months later, he contacted an uncle in Wichita, Kansas, because he again wanted something other than what he was doing. He wanted a new job, more freedom and opportunity. His uncle told him to come, and he did. He bought an airline ticket with his chicken money and soon, at his uncle's insistence, started high school.

Other than those years in the Buddhist temple, he'd never had any education, so American high school seemed impossible. Now, he wishes he had listened to his uncle's advice and stayed in school, but back then, in 1982, just twenty years old, what seemed clear to him was that high school was impossible. He couldn't understand a thing. "I cannot handle it," he told his uncle. "I don't want to go to school—I want to work." His uncle's sponsor got him a job in a propane factory.

It was during this time, for the first time in his life, that a twenty-year-old who'd become a man on his own, attended a Christian church.

It was during this time, for the first time in his life, that a twenty-year-old who'd become a man on his own, attended a Christian church. His uncle's sponsors wanted them to come to worship, so his uncle went dutifully, even though he understood nothing and didn't believe a bit of it. It was a matter of courtesy. But Keo owed his uncle's sponsors nothing, so after a visit or two, he told his uncle he wouldn't go back. It made no sense. Besides, the son of a spiritist father and Buddhist mother had no time for whatever bizarre stuff went on in that strange place.

Slowly, Keo Phommarath was meeting other Laotians and hearing about places where jobs were plentiful and pay was healthy. Soon he moved to Grand Island, Nebraska, where he found a woman—many women, actually—and started living the kind of wild life he'd been into just a few years before in Thailand.

The old ways

By this time, it's clear that Keo Phommarath is a fighter. When he left his village for the first time at just thirteen years old, he was pushed into an adult world where his own livelihood depended upon his guts, his heart, and his strength. He didn't need a savior; he'd saved himself. He was a fighter, and what characterized his life from that time on—from the day he moved to Grand Island until the day he found the Lord—is a spirit of selfishness that's not all that far from an American vision. He was going to get all he could out of life, all of its pleasures, all of its celebrity. He wanted to be an action hero, the party king, the guy everybody wanted to know. Music was his thing, the keyboard his instrument of choice. He was in a band, in the clubs, at all of the parties.

"I was all on my own," he says, "and I fell back into that old way of life—I was cheating on my girlfriend. I had fun and got crazy. I beat up people—white people, too. I beat up my girlfriend until she couldn't handle me anymore, and she left. Then I got even more crazy."

He arrived, terrifyingly, at the bottom, the very bottom, of his life in a place named Liberal, Kansas, where he found a woman he liked, someone he wanted to stay with, someone he wanted for longer than a night. But her father didn't like him, didn't trust him, didn't appreciate the fact that this wild musician kid—he was twenty-three years old—had no verifiable means of support. When her father denied his daughter to him, Keo Phommarath says he almost killed him.

If you listen to Keo tell his life's story, you might be surprised at how easily so much of it is related, as if his behavior were little more than normal, late-adolescent shenanigans. But this particular event, whatever it was that happened between the father of a girl he wanted and him is something he describes while looking away, in a kind of reverent fear for what nearly happened. "My temper was really very, very hot," he admits, and Boonjun, his wife, nods in agreement when he tells it. "I almost did something at that time that would have meant I would spend the rest of my life in jail."

He had to leave Liberal, Kansas, and friends said there were jobs in Sioux City, Iowa. He listened.

Boonjun's story

But before he left Kansas, he had met a woman named Boonjun, and she has been the only woman in his life for the past sixteen years. They met at a party, and at first, he says, she seemed to him nothing more or less than just another girl, another in an endless string of girls for him to please and to please him.

She was Thai, not Lao, and older than he was. But there was something about her that attracted him almost immediately, in a way that most other women hadn't; something in her made him want to know her better. And when, a few dates later, they sat together through a long night, talking, she told him the story of her life, how she'd once fallen in love with an American soldier in Thailand, how she'd bounced all over Europe and Asia with him as he was transferred after leaving Thailand. And she told him much more—how, at this man's request, she'd come to America to get ESL training so she could be his wife in *this* country, how she'd left her homeland to learn about the country where she was going to live once he left the military. But most unforgettably, Keo heard her talk, in tears, about having been abandoned. She was here, learning English, but he never reappeared. She never heard from that American soldier again.

She was alone, and that's what Keo heard most sharply. She had no one else in the world, nothing. Like him, in a way, she couldn't go back because there was really nothing to go back to. Unlike him, she had no memory at all of her mother, nothing. She was only a year old when her mother died in childbirth.

Really, Boonjun was homeless. She'd come from Germany, where she'd lived with her American soldier. She'd lived there both before and after some time spent in England. Her life in Thailand seemed so long ago that there seemed to be no reason for her to return there anymore. She was just a motherless, adopted child anyway. She had nothing—just a passport to come to the States, but nothing that would allow her to stay. She couldn't remain in the States without hiding, but she couldn't go anywhere else in the world, either. What broke his heart, he says, was hers, broken as his so often was. "When she told me everything," he remembers, "I cried inside my own heart."

Even today, when Boonjun tells her story, she frequently needs to dab at the tears that form at the corners of her eyes. "My life was terrible," she says. That's all.

> **Buddhism is a marvelously accommodating faith. It would not have dawned on either of them that they needed to discard anything of what they already were to become something else.**

By the time they moved to Sioux City, they had moved in together.

It was Boonjun who began the drift toward Christianity. Like Keo, she was, by her own profession, a Buddhist. But her faith didn't keep her from living with other faiths.

Buddhism is a marvelously accommodating faith. It would not have dawned on either of them that they needed to discard anything of what they already were to become something else.

Boonjun had attended Roman Catholic mass when she was living in England, and she loved the beauty of the cathedral and the rituals, even though she had no idea what was really happening inside. When a friend invited her to a church in Sioux City, she agreed, knowing nothing about what was going on there, either. What she wouldn't forget about that first visit, however, was that the people at worship actually prayed for her, asked God to find some relief for her from her asthma. When she left worship that first day, she says she felt better and, therefore, wanted to go again.

"If she wanted to go to church, that was fine with me," Keo says. "I had my own kinds of fun." Once he even went along and said all he got out of it was a headache. "I didn't have a clue what they were talking about."

Some time later, in fact, Boonjun was baptized, immersed totally, she says—and when she explains, she holds her nose as though just coming out of the water. She says she really didn't understand the Christian faith at the time, and the Buddhist icons and images that had always graced their apartment walls didn't come down, in spite her now being part of a local Christian church. Faith was, after all, simply a matter of gaining supernatural help for problems. What all religions share, she assumed, was access to communication with the spirit world, a world of love and care.

In 1998, an enterprising Lutheran pastor asked Keo if he and his musical group would lead the music in the church where many Lao people worshiped. The offer was, to Keo, perfectly acceptable, another gig—and they'd be paid, too. So he did it, starting a relationship that went on for almost two years, playing and singing every Sunday in a Christian worship service he knew nothing about, often high on drugs as he stood at his keyboard on stage, sunglasses masking his red eyes.

But it was that fragile connection—the music—that pushed him to consider God the Father Almighty. Even though Keo had never shown a moment's interest in the Christian faith, that same preacher wanted him to go with others to Winnipeg, Canada, to attend a conference of many Laotian Christians, Lao people from all over the world—North America, France, and even Laos.

"I was unemployed," he says. He'd been fired from his job at IBP (Iowa Beef Processors) because he'd beaten up his boss. "The preacher told me they would pay for my hotel and my food."

What he stumbled into in a big church in Winnipeg, Manitoba, Canada, was a throng of Laotian Christians, arms raised, some crying, others seemingly screaming to the Lord. It seemed, at first, like madness. "I wondered if I'd come to the wrong place," he says. "I thought to myself, 'These people are worshiping evil or else they're just crazy.'"

But what moved him profoundly was the mystery: why were these people doing what they were doing? What on earth was going on? He says he wanted badly to talk to someone, to discover what he had no way of understanding.

> What he stumbled into in a big church in Winnipeg, Manitoba, Canada, was a throng of Laotian Christians, arms raised, some crying, others seemingly screaming to the Lord. It seemed, at first, like madness.

That night, after the celebration, he went back to the hotel and met, for the first time, Khay Baccam. "I started to question him right away," he says. "I had just met him there, but I wanted to know what was happening."

They talked about Jesus Christ, talked all night long, Keo Phommarath; his friend, Sone; Khay Baccam; and another man, who like Keo had no idea about this God and his Son, Jesus. They talked all night long about the Christian God and Jesus the Messiah.

"When Khay told me about Jesus—about doing his work and all the stuff he knew," Keo says, "I compared the gospel to the Buddhist way."

That comparison, more than anything else in those long

hours of the night, made sense.

"You know, Buddhists are searching for the Messiah, too — we are searching for the Messiah." He draws the lines with his fingers as he explains. "Khay told me that this Jesus *is* the real Messiah." He shakes his head as if it remains incredible. "I was a Buddhist. I was a monk in the temple — and it's all very powerful to me and always had been." He shakes his head. "But in Jesus Christ, I found what I was looking for."

Even today, five years later, remembering that evening's all-night session nearly takes his breath away. "At the time, the Holy Spirit must have been calling me, telling me what to believe, you know — I can't remember it all exactly, but he must have been working in me, okay? — because that night, I accepted Jesus Christ as my Lord and Savior. That very night, in the all-night talking."

Something had changed forever in him, and somehow he knew it, even if his partying friends didn't and even if Boonjun, his wife, had no idea what had gone on in a church she'd never seen in Winnipeg.

Not long after, in the company of a pastor, he took down all of Boonjun's Buddhist artifacts, carried them out back of the only apartment they'd lived in since coming to Sioux City, and burned everything. His wife was furious — what he'd destroyed were mementos as well as sacred images, bits of what little she knew of family.

Keo asked Khay Baccam to come and explain to her, and Khay did, in another long night of story and sermon and acceptance. "He explained the Lord Jesus to her, and she believed, too," he says, sitting beside her on the couch in their new home close to downtown in Sioux City.

Keo's story is a long trip away and a long trip back. Remember the thirteen-year-old boy, all by himself on the quiet flow of the Mekong River, waiting for dangerous passage? He's going to a place he has no image of; he doesn't even know what a refugee camp is. He's all alone. He's got to make his own way. If he's to survive, he's going to have to trust himself. When he needs extra help, he prays to the Buddha whose ways he learned in those four years he spent in the temple.

That boy grew into a man by butting heads with whatever difficulties life rolled up in his way. He became a man with his fists. He swaggered through years of drugs and alcohol and parties he called "fun." He was guilty of things many Christians can barely imagine. He pulled himself up by his own bootstraps, only to be cut off at the knees by a God he never once expected to be capable of reining him in. In 1998, Keo Phommarath became something he'd never ever dreamed of becoming, a Christian believer.

Back to Laos

Even though he didn't "return" to faith, the path of his story circles back once more to Southeast Asia, to Laos, when, in 2001, he heard from his family that his mother was dying. With the help of many believers, he was able to fly back to see her, this woman who'd cried when her husband commanded her boys to leave the country, this woman who wanted him back so passionately that she was willing to throw herself to her death rather than return home without him.

His mother was dying. By grace, he'd been offered the chance to see her again, to talk to her in the name of Jesus Christ. And when he did, he told her about what was in his heart now—this new faith in this Messiah, this Jesus Christ.

Her son, Keo, had not become the monk she wanted him to be, but he'd become a stronger believer than either of them could have ever imagined. Before he left her side, and just before she died, his mother told him that she believed in the Lord Jesus Christ.

Today, Keo Phommarath leads Lao Unity Christian Reformed Church in Sioux City, Iowa. His joy and his blessed burden is to bring the gospel of light to the host of Laotian people in the region who have no ears for the music that now plays in his heart and soul.

"The Laotian people—just a small percentage are Christian," he says. "You know, I went to church first with my uncle in Wichita, Kansas—and I should have known God was there. But it's not easy. It's not your language, you know? Today, we preach in the Laotian tongue so everyone can understand what we're saying. Today, that is what we are doing, with God's help."

Where there were once many women, now there is one, Boonjun. Where there was so much drinking, now there is only the blood of our Lord. Where there once was song, now it is sheer praise to a Savior who took him from darkness and led him to the light of joy and peace in God's own love.

Neither Keo nor Boonjun are alone anymore. Thank the Lord, no, never alone.

BOUNMA AND
BOUPHANH SISOMBATH

....

What Can't Be Imagined
And What Can Be Believed

It's probably fair to say that an understanding of the lives of Bounma and Bouphanh Sisombath lies well outside the imaginative reach of most of their neighbors in Circle Pine, Minnesota, a northeastern suburb of the Twin Cities. But then, the story of their lives is well beyond the imagination of most North Americans. That they can live, today, so comfortably in their well-kept mobile home is a testimony to their courage and will and to the love of their heavenly Father.

Both of them were born in northeastern Laos, close to Vietnam, to families who kept themselves alive by subsistence farming. *Subsistence* is a fancy word that may well gloss over the reality of a difficult way of life. Try to imagine plowing the earth with a four-foot chunk of tree branch—no tractor, no spring-tooth plows, no oxen, no horses, no water buffalo.

Imagine scratching the soil with a stick.

Imagine a jungle, then think of burning it and cutting down what remains without the aid of a cherry-picker, a bulldozer, or even a chain saw. Imagine pulling stumps by hand, a long steel pole as a lever. Now, once again, imagine clearing a jungle by hand, then pulling out a stick to scratch the soil for a furrow. And don't think of the topography of northeast Laos as flat.

The backbreaking work required by peasant families in Laos and Thailand, in Cambodia and Vietnam, created much more than weary backs and broken hands. Bouphanh comes from a family of fourteen children; five of them never made it into their teenage years. Bounma's parents had eight children; he was the seventh. Six of them died young, most of malaria. There was no hospital, no medicine — there was only work and sometimes rice; there was always death.

Imagine a jungle neighborhood with no school. Bouphanh claims today that she grew up in a world without childhood. Life meant work. The Lao government had no money for schools. She had, she says, no time even to have a friend because she was constantly caring for her own family. Subsistence farming may well conjure up images of a sweet balance between human need and nature's beneficence. But in Thailand in the 1950s, the precarious balance most difficult to maintain was that fought for life itself, in the face of death's monstrous appetite, which left dark and empty spaces in every family.

Animism

Most North Americans have no way to imagine the nature of the religious faith that ran deeply through the consciousness of Laotian peasants. After all, there were no churches down the block; there were no blocks, only steep and craggy countryside where once there had been jungle.

Bounma's mother was the spiritual leader of the village where he grew up, where the people worshiped the spirit of the mountain, the spirit of the jungle, and the spirits of animals. The faith Bounma's mother dispensed to those who would visit their home is considered by some anthropologists to be humankind's original form of spirituality. Generally speaking, that religion is called animism, the belief that personal spiritual beings and impersonal spiritual forces have undeniable power over human affairs. Because they do, say the animists, every moment of a person's life — planting crops, conquering illness, getting married, moving away, having a child — requires those who believe to determine exactly what spiritual beings and forces might be affecting them.

Bounma remembers parents coming to his house for his mother's help because they believed that she knew how to speak to the spirits that may have been possessing their sick children; they believed that she could chase those spirits away by means of sacrificial offerings. By way of her communication with the afflicting spirits, Bounma's mother could determine exactly how much sacrifice the sickness required — a chicken maybe, a goat, or even a cow. With that sacrifice, the spirit would leave the sickly child and enter the animal to be slaughtered.

There's too much science in most of us to even imagine that kind of faith.

Bounma remembers late night rituals that seem, even now, he says, to be scary — like Halloween, he says, like *Dracula*. Midnight jungle darkness was the backdrop his mother's work required because no light could be shown during sacrifice. The only way most of us can even imagine such things is to cull images from nightmares.

Few of us can imagine a world where any and all political action requires greasy palms. When the government demanded taxes, Bounma's family risked forced labor — his father's having to clear more jungle to build roads. They fled one day's walk away (who among us can imagine distance between two villages measured simply by "one day's walk"?) to the village where Bouphanh lived with her family, a village where Bounma's uncle determined, with some strategic under-the-table payments, that no taxes would be required for his relative's family.

For most of us, it is impossible to imagine an arranged marriage; but if you want to know Bounma and Bouphanh Sisombath, you really should understand that their becoming man and wife was the result of parental matchmaking. Their story holds no dreamy romance, no cow eyes, no first kisses. The two families simply spoke together, Bouphanh's father pointing out to Bounma's parents what was already obvious: they had a daughter. Bounma's father likely nodded, smiling, and pointed to his eligible son. Bounma was twenty, Bouphanh eighteen.

Their story holds no dreamy romance, no cow eyes, no first kisses.

It goes without saying, one assumes, that no one in the entire region subscribed to *Brides* magazine or worried about which photographer would shoot the wedding. No travel agents sought the cheapest fares for a Vegas honeymoon.

That their marriage has lasted through poverty, war, refugee camps, and immigration is, by North American perceptions, incredible. Yet their relationship is stronger and more resilient than tens of thousands of others undertaken at the same time, half of which, statistically, have long ago dissolved.

Imagine a society where the best life possible is offered by the military. If a man wants to make a decent living, he joins the army, despite the fact that, for the most part, war is all around as it has been for years, the country hopelessly divided into three warring political forces. You fight the enemy or you fight poverty.

A year before he and Bouphanh were married, Bounma had joined the centrist forces in Laos. Soon after, the centrists had joined the right-wing when the left had joined the communist insurgency, and Bounma was in the middle of the war, a day's walk from the village where he'd married his new bride.

Try to imagine a war in which daily battles take place just a county away, so close that the combatants can walk home once night falls and the smoke clears.

When their village was overrun by the enemy in 1963, the only way Bounma could see his wife and family was by stealing across enemy lines. One night, he came to her bedroom and asked if she wanted to go with him—if the whole family would come, even the children. Bouphanh couldn't decide, because leaving with her husband, her baby in tow, would be very dangerous. Bounma's mother intervened. "You must go," she told her daughter-in-law.

The next night, when Bounma returned, accompanied by one of his friends, both of them slipping past the enemy in the middle of the night, the baby was strapped over Bouphanh's back in a makeshift knapsack. They were ready to leave on a three-day's walk back to Bounma's regiment.

And they were not alone. Bounma's mother came with them, as did his brother and sister, because life would have been difficult, if not impossible for them under communist rule. By the next morning, it had become clear that their son and brother was the enemy and that his wife had been stolen away.

Try to imagine the silhouettes of six shadowy figures, one of them carrying a baby, up against a moonlit riverbank.

Sometime before Bounma's return, Bouphanh's mother, concerned about her daughter's safety, had told her that because her husband had gone to war, she should assume that he would never return. The communists all around would make it impossible.

But the morning after six shadowy figures slipped silently out the village, Bouphanh's mother found the house completely empty. The wailing she began at that moment alarmed the communist forces, who sent troops to find the trail of those who'd left, to bring them back—or kill them.

One left behind

If you can, imagine a dark-of-night jungle scene, mountainous terrain, and listen for the sound of communist soldiers behind you as you try to find the kind of footing that will keep you moving fast enough to stay out front of death. Bounma's brother was sick, as was his sister, very sick, with malaria, but there was no possibility of slowing down. Jungle trails were barely recognizable. With any hint of someone lurking, they took cover and tried to keep the baby still.

They couldn't follow the river. Bounma knew the path at the edge was planted with landmines and strung with booby-traps. The next day—and there had been no sleep because they had to keep going—they came to a war-torn deserted village. Bounma's sister, burning with fever and gravely ill, could not keep pace. They did what they could to try to keep her alive, but they knew they were being closely followed.

It is not something they like to remember, but neither is what happened next something they can easily forget. Bounma's sister died that day in that deserted village, and under cover of darkness, they buried her quickly before, once again, moving on.

This is not a movie script, not a TV special. Somewhere beneath the damp earth of what was once a jungle village in northeast Laos lie the remains of Bounma's sister, another of his siblings who never made it to adulthood. When finally they entered the camp of the friendly forces, there were only five shadowy figures—tired and hungry.

For two more years, Bounma stayed in the army, fighting the communists beside Hmong peasant guerillas. For two years, the battles raged—men and women died, were slaughtered, were buried. For two years, only occasionally did Bounma see Bouphanh, who had been taken to safety in a nearby city. In those two years, another child was born before the communists overran the place where Bouphanh had thought she would be safe.

Always, Bounma was at war, killing in order not to be killed. War was his occupation, daily jungle battles as regular as a factory job. Whenever the fighting ceased, he would leave the front lines and stay with Bouphanh, who, like many other wives, stayed with her children within a day's walk of the war, her husband a commuter soldier.

And then things changed. When their third child was soon

to be born, the entire family was sent to Vientiane, where Bouphanh could get good medical treatment. For the first time in several years, they found themselves safely outside harm's way. They had two children, and, there in Vientiane, a third on the way, it suddenly seemed wrong for them to go back to war. Bounma had spent too many years in the jungle, fighting. They simply didn't return.

It may be difficult to imagine that his leaving the military could be accomplished so easily, but it wasn't hard because Bounma had no permanent address, no passport, no green card, no driver's license, no social security. There was no way to track down Cpl. Bounma Sisombath, to find him or his family and to bring him back to the front.

They had two children, and, there in Vientiane, a third on the way, it suddenly seemed wrong for them to go back to war.

Even though he knew that leaving the military meant its own kind of hardship—fighting men lived better than peasants, after all—he decided to disappear into the civilian world, the world he'd left when he became a soldier years before.

But outside the military, the battle to provide for his family became, in a way, more intense. For a time, he sold bread—bought it from a factory, then peddled it on city streets from the back of a bicycle.

A year after their third child was born, the Sisombath family moved to Langchan, Hmong territory, where the local economy was thriving because of the presence of the American CIA. For four years, from 1968 to 1972, Bounma made a living as a construction worker, building a new dam north of Vientiane. But conditions were primitive in terms of medical care; what little medicine there was came only via the black market. Their new baby died there one night, victim of a raging fever.

For the next eight years, Bounma tried hard to feed his growing family, at first by farming in the old way, then, once the communists took over, by clearing jungle once again. Leaving

Laos behind seemed the only way to provide for them, but he and Bouphanh knew that the first step would be to get back to Vientiane, and closer, thereby, to the Mekong River and Thailand. For a year, Bounma lived in the capital city but traveled up close to the Vietnam border to sell tape recorders and watches to the Vietnamese people. By this time, there were nine children—"so many kids and so many mouths to feed," Bounma remembers.

What's more, he found himself responsible for two nephews and his mother, a total of fifteen people in a sprawling extended family.

Bouphanh's parents had left Laos for the United States in 1980, and now Bounma and Bouphanh wanted to escape, too; there was nothing left in Laos—no freedom, no work, no social security, no welfare—nothing to help them raise their big family. There was, quite simply, no future. What's more, they had to pay taxes on a very limited income, and Bounma's life was forever in danger since he'd once served in the opposition's army.

Even though escaping Laos in 1980 wasn't as terrifying as it may have been a decade earlier, one couldn't slip over a border easily in the company of fifteen people, more than half of them children. In some ways, though, getting to Thailand was more expensive than it was dangerous.

It took lots of money to pay the old friend of his who set up the escape, as well as the authorities on the other side who also required a share. What it cost was 7,000 Thai baht, over three hundred U.S. dollars back then, to find a means by which to bring fifteen people out of Laos and into Thailand.

In November 1981, with enough money to pay everything required, they crossed over the Mekong River into Thailand.

Christianity

For three years, the whole Sisombath family lived in Thai refugee camps, where a good deal of the food that came from the United Nations was gobbled up by supervisors before what was left trickled down to the poorest of the poor. Bounma tried to do business in the camp at Nong Khai, selling charcoal or wood for fires, using whatever few dollars he could make to feed his large family.

There, in the camps, in the early 1980s, Bounma and Bouphanh first encountered this strange new religion called Christianity. At first, it was the Catholics. Not long after came the Seventh-Day Adventists; two of the Sisombath boys started hanging out at an Adventist ministry designed for kids.

With all of those mouths to feed and little wherewithal to get the job accomplished, Bounma found something he needed in Christianity. Whatever its peculiar flavor, the Christian faith became synonymous with *help*. Camp residents claimed that if you wanted to get to America, you should go to the Christians and join because the Christians could get you there much faster.

Among the Adventists, Bounma learned something about prayer in the new religion: if he would ask this Christian God for something, whatever he would ask for would be given him. That was the promise.

It seemed, of course, too good to be true. But what possible problem could arise from simply asking this God, he thought.

So he did. The first prayers he offered to the God of the Holy Scriptures, a God he will tell you today he didn't really know at all, had to do with his family, his big, big family. In the camps in Thailand, then again in the Philippines, he closed his eyes and asked this God for help in relocating his large family to the United States. He asked God not simply for a passage to America, but for the opportunity to help his children have good lives.

It's quite likely that most of the Sisombath's neighbors in Circle Pine, Minnesota—most of us probably—will have no problem understanding the nature of Bounma's very first prayers, for they were, quite simply, the prayers of any concerned father or mother. He wanted a good home for his family. Not just once did he ask, he says, but time and time again.

Those prayers, offered to God many times through the next several years, were answered, as promised, when in 1985 the entire extended family was given permission to emigrate to the United States, to Minnesota, where they were sponsored by Bouphanh's parents, who had come five years earlier.

Bounma admits that although those prayers were offered—and answered—he really wasn't a believer in Jesus Christ. Today, both he and his wife laugh when they remember how little they understood at the time, at the image of a man who used the Christian faith as he would have used anything else at the time to secure a means by which to better himself and offer his children the possibility of a better future.

Bounma had begun going to church with the Adventists, but Bouphanh didn't like this odd and strange new practice, and she told him so. More importantly, she didn't like him acting—she didn't like her husband being a liar. Even so, often she would accompany him because, after all, he was her husband and it was her role to do what he wanted.

Life in Minnesota was an unimaginable change. Bounma was uneducated and had trouble reading his own Laotian language. American officials told him that he had few job skills in this new culture; what's more, he had a huge family. Maybe his job, they told him, should be to raise his children, to love them, to help them, to be, first and foremost, a parent, a father.

Bounma says that that advice was very confusing to him. In Laos and then in the camps, he had to work very hard to get so very little. Once here, he and his family found themselves being helped by many people, including many Christians, and his own life changed dramatically: he didn't have to work as hard, and, strangely enough, there was always enough. Life was confusing, but it was also clear that his prayers—the first ones he'd offered up to this Christian God—were somehow being miraculously answered.

New prayers in a new world

Once here, Bounma's prayers began to change, because he recognized—as did so many other Asian immigrants at that time—that raising his children in a big city in the United States was not easy. The oldest was just eighteen when they arrived, and there were, after all, eight children behind him.

Keeping them safe and in line in this new culture demanded wholly different skills from the ones he would have had to use in Laos. Once again, he began to pray. "I'm not a very smart man, Lord," he said. "I cannot speak English—and sometimes it's very hard for me to read even the Lao language. But I pray that you will help me to live with my kids—keep them from the gangs, the killing, and the drugs, the bad things that happen in the United States."

That's what he asked of the Lord.

And once again, he says, the Lord answered him. Never, he says, were any of his children into gangs. They lived in downtown Minneapolis at the time, but their children never entered into a life that brought so many other Asian immigrants so much pain. Bounma had only one way of understanding why—it was this God people talked about and prayed to, this God who, he says, had sent him a miracle. "That showed me," he says, "the power of the Lord."

While it may be difficult for those of us who know Bounma and Bouphanh to imagine the world from which they came, those of us who know the Lord Jesus Christ will have far less of a problem understanding what happened to them when they came to him as Savior. At this point, *their* story—which begins so far from American cities and streets—begins to look more and more like all of ours, if we know him.

Even though Bounma and his wife and children regularly attended worship at a series of churches, most of them Lao, his wife of so many years was not happy, she says. She still thought her husband to be a liar, a man who was using the Christian faith to get what he wanted and needed.

It would take a third series of intense prayers for her to be convinced that he had found something deeply important in this new religion. To understand that change, we need to return to Laos and Thailand, the soldier's life, life in the camps, life as a man in the old country.

With all of those children to feed, with all of the work he took on to keep his family safe and healthy, with all of the fighting, the death and destruction, Bounma Sisombath, like many others, he says, had lived a life too full of seaminess—more drinking, more smoking, more gambling than he could afford. Once here in the States, that didn't change. He may well have been praying fervently for his family, but his own behavior was not at all exemplary—and she knew it. That's why she thought that he was lying. While he was attending church and praying to the Lord, he was living a life that made her believe all his sincere religiosity was nothing but a show.

He may well have been praying fervently for his family, but his own behavior was not at all exemplary—and she knew it. That's why she thought that he was lying.

So the third series of intense prayers, he says, was his asking God to help him escape the smoking, the drinking, the gambling, the carousing that was part of a way of life that hadn't changed, even in this new land.

Amid the prayers—and the answers to prayers—Bounma says he became ashamed of himself; he wanted to become someone he'd never been, in part because of the way in which his own intense prayers were actually being answered. The family was here, after all—his children were doing well. He wasn't proud of himself for the card games he spent too much time playing, and he often hid his smoking from his Christian friends. He says he didn't enjoy anymore the booze that was offered him.

He asked the Lord, he says, to make him quit. "Please make me sick," he prayed, "so I cannot smoke anymore because I think my lungs are sick." And he prayed for an end to drinking and gambling, too. Once more, the Lord delivered.

"Many people, even if they are strong Buddhists, cannot get out of the way they live," he says today, "but I did because God has the power to take me out of a way of life too many of my friends couldn't get out of."

And that change—his becoming responsible about his own life—was the change that Bouphanh couldn't miss in her husband. There was something in this new Christian faith that made him a better man, a better husband, a better father. Something profound and wonderful had happened to the man who'd once rescued her and her baby from a village full of the enemy; he'd been rescued himself by someone she thought that she needed to know.

A changed husband

Bounma's conversion to the Christian faith and a more responsible life made clear to her that he wasn't just playacting. Something made him stronger and more loving. She had frequently accompanied her husband to whatever church he was attending, but she began to pay attention to what was being preached and practiced only when something about that faith changed the man she loved. That conversion—her conversion—she says took about fifteen years from the time her husband first began to pray to this new God and his Son, Jesus Christ.

But when it did come, finally, it created another miracle. Like her husband, Bouphanh had never gone to school as a child, never learned to read. There were no schools for people that poor. After her conversion, she, too, began to pray earnestly for a special gift. All around her, in worship, she noticed the very special joy other believers took from singing praises to the God who had saved them—and her husband, and now her. She couldn't sing. Even though the language on the page was her native Lao tongue, she had no access to those words. They weren't part of her childhood; they were part of a wholly new way of life, even though the words themselves were in a tongue she understood.

For months and months, she studied what she saw on the page as she listened to words from the mouths and souls of the people around her. She asked the Lord, time and time again, for the ability to read those words so as to sing, with the others, her own praises. "Lord," she said, "I know you're there. I want to praise you with my heart and my song, but I cannot read."

And then, miraculously, she says, it happened: what had seemed little more than scratchings of a pen formed into the very words she was hearing. "Now," she says, "I can read, and I pray every night."

Few of us, if any, can wrap our imaginations around miracles.

Today, Bounma and Bouphanh Sisombath, the children of Laotian peasants, lead others to the faith that, by their own testimony, has changed them. By definition uneducated and illiterate, they have discovered the wisdom that transcends all limitations and today stand before other believers—and those not yet accepting of the Christian faith—and testify, in words and deeds, to the great goodness of God's grace.

It may well be impossible for their own neighbors—for that matter, for their American brothers and sisters in the Lord—to imagine what kind of life Bounma and Bouphanh led so many thousands of miles away in a place so many Christian believers in this country don't even know exists. Animal sacrifice, arranged marriage, subsistence farming with a stick, life-or-death escapes, and fifteen family members in a refugee camp waiting patiently for a new life—theirs is a wholly different kind of story than most can tell.

But today, the Sisombaths sit at the same table, the Lord's

table, with many, many thousands, even millions of Christian believers around the world; and those who know the Lord, as they do, have no trouble whatsoever understanding the most dramatic chapter of their miraculous pilgrimage because, like all of us, once they were lost, but now they've been found by the Light of the world, a Savior named Jesus Christ, our Lord.

No matter where we spent our childhood or how our histories are written, that chapter in every believer's story — God's love for us — is always and for all time, the very same.

SOMPHET SOUTHAYA

A Story of Prayers Answered

"Sometimes on my own time, I try to reach people and tell them about Jesus Christ," says Somphet Southaya. He lives in Sioux City, Iowa, on a pleasant street in Morningside, a southeast suburb of the city. He is talking about friends, Lao friends, and there are thousands in Sioux City, only a tiny fraction of them believers in Jesus Christ. "Sometimes they don't understand how Christ saves us, you know? They hear that Jesus Christ was born two thousand years ago. 'Only two thousand years ago, and he's God?' they say, 'Buddha was born first!' They say that."

The birth date of Jesus Christ is only one problem of many in communicating the gospel to Lao people. "They don't know that Jesus Christ was born to save us from our sin, to die on the cross for us because we don't obey God." That's a difficult lesson to teach people to whom the Christian gospel is completely new, especially when that gospel concerns a God they believe to be younger than Buddha.

What Phet has to tell his Lao friends is that Christ is only one part of the Godhead. "God the Father was always there— you know, from the beginning." That's what he tells them. "They say, 'God was born only two thousand years ago.' So I try to explain to them, 'God was always there—from the beginning he was there. He's always there.'"

You might say that Phet's own life is proof of his testimony of God's always being there for his people. You might say that Phet knows what he is talking about because God has always been there in his own life. You might say that even though there were times when Phet himself wasn't interested in knowing whether God was in the neighborhood, the eternal God was always there, watching him.

Somphet Southaya, the fifth of nine children of Nou Southaya, was born in Vientiane, the capital of Laos, where he lived for his first eight years while his father was a captain in the Laotian army. After the communist Pathet Lao took control of Laos in 1975 and abolished the monarchy, Phet's father, like thousands of military men of the former government, was regarded as dangerous to the new regime and sent to a "seminar camp," many of which were known only by their numbers.

"My father knew it was going to happen," Phet says. The authorities told him that to receive his salary, he was going to have to go where they told him. They sent him to a camp in Senquon, northern Laos, at first alone, apart from his family.

Not long after, the family received a note from their father. "Come and see me," he wrote, but Phet knows now that his father could not tell his family the truth about where he was

Phet says that he quickly began to understand that his father was not a free man but a prisoner.

or what he was doing. The younger children—six in all, Phet the oldest of them—left with their mother to visit, first taking a troop truck, then a boat, in a trip that took several days. What they found was a lonely, recently constructed jungle outpost, but when the officials in charge took his father from his barracks and gave the family a separate room, things seemed to be working out quite well.

Perceptions changed. Day after day, they watched their father work hard, very hard, digging into the root-infested jungle earth for hours, sometimes for what appeared to be no good reason. Phet says that he quickly began to understand that his father was not a free man, but a prisoner. In addition, there was never enough food—and what there was didn't sit well with Phet's family: steamed rice, not sticky rice.

Moving, again and again

The next five years of his life are a succession of moves, with his family, to isolated jungle camps, one after another on a slow crawl north. The operation was always the same. They would arrive at some remote place in the jungle where their father and the other ex-military would begin to clear trees and construct housing, then start again on the major project, a road that would eventually reach north to China. Food was always scarce, medical treatment minimal, freedom nonexistent. To help support his family, Phet remembers cutting branches for fishing poles, spending his boyhood trying to catch fish to bring home to eat.

In 1980, somewhere in the far north of Laos, his mother became gravely ill. "I'm going to die because I can't make it," she told the family. Malnutrition and near starvation had taken their toll, and the only way out—his father, told the camp officials—was a trip back to Vientiane, where he could get his wife to a doctor.

Surprisingly, the men in charge let them leave, put them on a big truck to return to the capital city, excused them because of his wife's illness. Even Phet's father could go; it was clear that he was in no position to take care of the small children.

"When you want to go back, just let us know," the truck driver said when he let the family off in Vientiane. What Phet's father knew the moment he left the camp was that he never, ever wanted to go back.

Once his wife was healthy, he and his family took advantage of the government's inattention and left Vientiane, heading south instead to his hometown, Kantao, a two-day boat trip from the capital city.

Phet was a boy, slowly becoming a man, and he remembers a certain amount of fear at that time because he was old enough to understand that his father's plans were contrary to what the government intended. "To my father, it was either go back to the camp or find a better life," he says. "We were taking a risk, but to us there was no choice."

The boat trip left them twenty miles from Kantao, and the only way to get home was to walk—so they did. He remembers carrying his sister. Phet Southaya was just twelve years old.

Emaciated, protein-deficient, thin as walking ghosts, seven members of the Southaya family arrived together, finally, at grandma's house. There was, as you can imagine, great rejoicing.

Following the Pathet Lao takeover in 1975, it had slowly become clear to Nou Southaya that if he and his family were ever going to have a chance to prosper, to live whole and healthy lives, he would have to consider leaving Laos and going to America. And it was there, at Kantao, his own ancestral home, that he finally made the decision to cross the shallow waters of the Mekong River and enter Thailand. It was there, in Thailand, that he knew he could get his family into a refugee camp and eventually set them on the road to a new life in a new world.

It would be easy to say that Jesus Christ was not yet a part of this story. After all, Phet's father was a Buddhist, although not a strong one. What Phet remembers of his father's religion is a little statue he took with him into war—not much more. Jesus Christ and the whole story of Jehovah, God the Father Almighty, was largely unknown to anyone in the Southaya family, the idea of their being Christian someday unimaginable. But what Phet now knows is that God is always there—

always has been and always will be.

It was at the Lao refugee camp in Nong Khai, Thailand, that Phet Southaya heard the very first word associated with the Christian religion, the word *church*. And it came up this way: other Lao people — refugees all — claimed that this thing called "the church" would help people. "That's all I knew," he says. In the camps, he attended once a month, but "I didn't understand at all what was going on."

He remembers a film of some type, put on by a missionary group who worked in the refugee camp in Nong Khai. "They had a film about Jesus, spoken in Lao — where he comes from, and what he was," he says. "At that time, we didn't know anything about Jesus Christ — we just went to church." But that film he remembers, probably because it related the gospel story in his native language.

After a long and frightening interview during which Thai officials needed to make sure that the Southaya family was Lao and not Thai, Phet and his family received permission to leave for the Philippines, where they entered yet another refugee camp, another step on their way to America. There, for the first time, they studied the English language and tried to get a handle on American culture while waiting for a sponsor from the United States. What Phet remembers is the language training especially, probably because he was, and still is, especially blessed with language skills. While others had headaches with the new and complicated English language, Phet loved the class. "She talked and we listened — and it was fun," he says.

When a sponsor was finally enlisted, his family left the camp in the Philippines by bus on a three-hour trip to Manila, where they boarded a plane that brought them to New York City about a day later. Most of the time on the plane, he says, he slept.

What he remembers best about his arrival was the number of African-American people he saw around him, numbers he'd never seen before. He was still a boy in many ways, of course, and he says he wondered at first if he was indeed in the United States. "Maybe we got on the wrong plane," he remembers thinking.

It was September 1981. Phet was fifteen years old, and he and four brothers and sisters, along with his mother and his father, suddenly found themselves in a small apartment — with no furniture to speak of — on the second floor of a building in a city called Brooklyn, New York.

He still doesn't know exactly what happened, but what he'll never forget is that, once they were in that barren apartment, the sponsor did little or nothing to help the Southaya family. Daily, he'd bring in some American food. But otherwise, they never saw the man. Soon enough, another refugee family — people they didn't know — was deposited in the little apartment, all of them scared to death of the new and completely foreign world around them. For two weeks, two families, just-arrived strangers in a very strange land, slept together on the bare floor.

> He still doesn't know exactly what happened, but what he'll never forget is that, once they were in that barren apartment, the sponsor did little or nothing to help the Southaya family.

When his father had had enough of the sponsor's inattention, he left the apartment on his own to look for other Lao people, found some, and soon determined that the best course of action would be to go to a place those people called "Rhode Island," where there was a Lao community that would help them. But how? And where was Rhode Island? No one had any idea.

Phet was the oldest child. He wandered out on the street himself one day and recognized somehow from a sign that a building just down the block was a "church." He asked a passerby, "Is this a church?" She told him yes. His own camp experience had taught him that *church* meant *help*, so he wandered in.

"Can I help you?" a woman asked him.

"Our family is living in an office for a couple of months already," he told her, in a language he knew only slightly. "We can't get out of there. We need some money to pay someone to take us to Rhode Island."

The helping place

The very next day, the woman came looking for them, found them, brought them food — and on Sunday came to bring them to *church*, the helping place. He remembers, too, his very first Bible study, conducted by the people in the Brooklyn church. "I wasn't sure at all where Jesus came from," he says. "But on Sunday night, the people from the church took us to a Bible study and talked about Genesis — where God comes from. That's how I became a Christian — the very first day."

Phet Southaya was still a boy really, and a child in faith, but already a child of God.

In time, the people from the church got the Southaya family out of the apartment and on their way to Rhode Island. From there, they eventually made their way to California, where a relative said there were good jobs to be had. In Fresno, Phet enrolled in his first American school, started tenth grade, and eventually graduated from high school — after a lot of hard work, he says — in 1987. In California, they attended Redeemer Lutheran Church faithfully, and he and all of the members of his family were baptized. "All of us are strong believers," he says, meaning all of his family, today.

But the story isn't over. Because of his abilities in language, he found himself in a position to help others in the Lao community, people who needed help with contracts, legal situations, and applications. One day, a woman came to him. She'd been married to an American who'd divorced her and taken custody of her child. She was trying to get visitation rights, and she needed legal help.

One thing led to another, and when Phet, then a college student at Fresno's City College, helped her secure the rights she was trying to attain, the two of them fell into a relationship, a relationship that eventually led him to leave his family and his church for Sioux City, Iowa. More importantly, that relationship kept Phet away from a growing relationship with Jesus Christ.

"If you take a burning stick out of the fire, it will stop burning," he explains. "It needs the rest of the fire to stay in flame."

They moved together, unmarried, to America's heartland, where both took jobs in local industry, Phet as a meat cutter with John Morrell and the woman at Iowa Beef Processors. They were living together, working hard, making money, establishing a life here in the country they'd been in for less than a decade, but they were doing all of that without the help of the Lord.

This is the way Phet explains what happened. "During the next ten years, I never felt good. My heart was upset almost all of the time, and I wasn't happy. I might be happy once in a while, but mostly I felt guilty." He shakes his head. "When I first met her, I didn't realize that would happen, but it did. I fell into something—I didn't know what I was falling into, really."

His companion didn't care for this word *church*, certainly not for the Christian religion into which he'd been growing. Often, in those early years, they'd argue. "Why should you go to church?" she would ask him. "You're just wasting your time. Why don't you just come with me to the casino?"

After all, stopping there was convenient—the casino's flashing lights were right along the streets he took to get home.

So he did. At first, once in awhile, then more and more often until finally, after a few years in Sioux City, he'd stop—with her or without her—almost every day on his way home from work. After all, stopping there was convenient—the casino's flashing lights were right along the streets he took to get home.

"In those ten years I started to gamble—you know," he says. "I walked away from God. I turned away from him."

Miraculously, however, God never walked away from him.

"I stopped going to church, and I started to gamble. I didn't lie to people, I didn't shoot people, I didn't cheat people—but I gambled a lot. I gambled a lot," he says.

Back in California, his parents were growing stronger and stronger in the Christian faith, and as they grew, their prayers for their son became more intense because they knew he was walking away from what little he knew about Jesus Christ. They knew he was abandoning the love that they were finding so real in their new Christian faith. "My parents prayed for me almost every day," he says. "They called me on the phone and said, 'How are you coming along?'" They'd tell their son, who'd left them and the faith, that they were putting their trust in the will of the Lord.

"And their prayers worked!" Phet says today. "They kept praying, kept praying, kept praying—for nine years they kept praying. Even when they didn't call me for a long time, they kept praying, and their prayers worked."

He and his girlfriend were addicted, he admits. They spent significant time and significant money at the casino almost every day. "I stopped all of the time," he says. "We lost a lot of money."

Then one day, he started wondering about everything. He asked himself what on earth he was living for. For the most part, he says, neither of them was noticing what they were doing, losing money day after day. Neither of them was even thinking about it.

Of course, it was easy to forget the path of his life when they'd win—and occasionally they would. "When you lose a lot, you think about it," he says, "but when you win, you never think about it." Now, out of the cycle, he can laugh a little at the trap of gambling. "I'd start to feel guilty, then win again and win again and forget everything."

But finally, in 1998, he'd had enough. It seemed to him that he'd been working hard in Sioux City, Iowa, for ten years and really, honestly, had accomplished nothing. It was an empty life he was living, despite the ringing joy of the casino's happy slot-machines and all of the bright lights. Really, truly — what had they done with their lives in those years? Nothing.

He told her he had to leave. He told her she could keep whatever it was they'd accumulated — the house, even his clothes. He knew he had to get out. "I got to thinking that God was calling me back to him, that he would forgive me for what I did and what I didn't do." What he told his companion was tough, and, in a way, he felt sorry for her. He'd lived with her for ten years and knew it would be painful to leave — but he had to. And now, when he looks back, what he sees is an escape from something that would have imprisoned him no less completely than his father in the camps of northern Laos. "God called me out — if he wouldn't have called me away from that relationship," he says, "I think I would have been stuck in it forever."

Today, three years later, in a house in Morningside, he sits on the couch beside Kao, his wife of two years, a fellow Christian, a woman he met at the Lao Lutheran Church once he left the casino and the woman he'd lived with for ten years. Today, their son Andrew, just one year old, laughs and plays on the living room floor in front of them. "God has blessed me," he says, "with a son, with this house, with a good job." Still at John Morrell, Phet is off the line now and in the packaging department, working with boxes, a job he likes.

"When we talk about our future," he says, looking at Kao, "we'd like to serve the Lord. Maybe even go to the Lao people. You know, many of them don't know the Lord. We would like to tell them about Jesus Christ."

Church means *help* — that's what he learned first in the camp in Thailand. Church meant food and clothing to people who had so very little.

But now, after almost twenty years in America, what it's come to mean to him is another kind of *help* — help with the sickness of the soul, help with despair and sadness, help out of a life that is going nowhere. Today, to Samphet Southaya, church means *Christ*, and Christ means *help* forever, for all time.

So when his Lao friends say that Jesus Christ is a latecomer when compared to Buddha, he tells them, "God was always there—from the beginning he was there. He's always there."

That's not just something he's been told. It's something he knows down deep in his soul. Even though Somphet had left God, *that* God was always there.

He is always there.

SONE DEDTHANOU

··

Finding *the* Messiah

When Deuane Ksopsmopsou, of South Sioux City, Nebraska, began to show an interest in the Christian faith, Pastor Khay Baccam invited him, like many others, to a Bible study where he could learn more about Jesus Christ and the promises of his love. What he learned there both surprised and fascinated him. Later, when he was convinced of the truth that the Bible teaches, he turned his life over to the Lord.

But what shocked Deuane Ksopsmopsou at one of those first Bible studies was walking into a room and spotting a familiar face, a man he remembered from Laos, someone he could never easily forget.

There, behind the table, sat a man named Sone Dedthanou. Deuane could not believe his eyes. The Sone he remembered from Laos was not a man he would ever imagine would or could embrace the love of Jesus; the Sone Dedthanou that Deuane remembered was a gang leader given to violence, a man who wielded his significant authority like a lawless thug.

Afterward, Deuane approached Khay cautiously. "You know this man Sone very well?" he whispered.

Khay told him that he thought that he did know Sone and that he had known him for quite some time already.

"How long has he been a Christian?" Deuane asked.

"Maybe four or five years," Khay said. "Why? Do you know him, too?"

"Of course I know him," Deuane said, "and that's why I asked. How on earth did that happen?"

The miracle of grace

Nothing on earth, finally, is as miraculously shocking as grace. Nothing we will ever experience in this life comes close to the sheer wonder created by the power of God Almighty to take unto himself those he claims as his own. Deuane's slack-jawed astonishment at seeing Sone Dedthanou, of all people, studying the Christian scripture is itself a testimony to the astonishing reality of God's love and mercy.

Today Sone Dedthanou pastors the Lao Church (Christian Reformed) of Worthington, Minnesota. Today, Pastor Sone Dedthanou still participates, weekly, in the Bible studies that have changed his life forever; today, in fact, he leads those Bible studies. He preaches the good news from a pulpit God has given him. Today, he helps his people with problems they face, day to day, in this new country, in its often bewildering culture. Today, when Lao parents worry about their children's behavior, afraid of the gangs that seem to rule many immigrant communities, Sone Dedthanou can, without blushing, tell them—and he does—that he knows, firsthand, the very worst that can happen; but he also understands, first-hand, how great is the love of the Father. He has been, after all, the astonished recipient of God's incredible grace.

To characterize Sone Dedthanou's life in Thailand as that of a lawless thug misses half of the story. There's much more to him and to his early years. He is sixty-one years old now, his face is square-jawed and strong, his eyes resolute and fearless. When he sits behind his pastor's desk in Worthington, he could still pass for a wrestler. Honestly, even today, he looks like a tough guy.

When he was just a boy, he met a Thai missionary who rode into his hometown, Say Fong, Thailand, on a motorcycle. All of the kids were excited, not so much to hear a Christian missionary as to see and hear an actual motorcycle. Most of the kids' parents wouldn't have approved of their listening to this missionary, he says, but then most of the parents were hard at work in nearby fields and never saw the man.

What Sone remembers about that single visit from a Christian is music, the songs this man sang as he accompanied himself on the guitar he had carried along over his back. He also remembers an odd idea this man told the children, the gospel's essence in one familiar line: "If you believe on the Lord Jesus Christ, you'll go to heaven."

Sone remembered that line because something about it struck his child's imagination as dead wrong. When he returned that night and spoke briefly to his father, his father thought that such an idea—that simply believing and doing nothing more would bring eternal reward—was woefully misguided and, what's worse, simply flat wrong.

His mother, on the other hand, was angry that the missionary had spoken to the kids, offended at the silliness of this bizarre faith, in part because of language. Central to the Jesus story, of course, is his mother, Mary. Sone's own mother wanted no part of being associated with the word *Mary*, a word she had no way of translating except as "dog-licked." Christians, she and others had thought, were somehow "dog-licked," and she certainly did not want her son—or any of her children—hanging around with dog-licked kids.

A religious home

But Christianity presented more than a language problem. His father's dismissal and his mother's derision are attributable in part to their own significant religious convictions and practices. Make no mistake, Sone Dedthanou was born into a deeply religious home. His father, he says, was a seeker, a man who spent most of his first twenty-five years at the temple, in training to become a monk. He was a student of Buddhist scriptures, a man who wanted, quite frankly, to believe everything—Buddhism, Hinduism, ancestor worship, and the reality of the spirit world. He wanted to embrace all faiths, each one of them, and in that quest came, sadly, to embrace none of them with heart, mind, and soul.

Sone explains that his father believed in everything to be sure that, should one faith prove eternally right, he'd have covered all of the bases. To the end of his life, Sone will tell you, his father remained a highly spiritual person, a seeker, someone who wanted badly to be sure of the exact reality of the supernatural world—a deeply spiritual man, but not particularly religious.

And it's interesting to know that when his father left the temple before actually becoming a Buddhist monk, he suffered the derision of the community; many people attributed his father's occasional bad harvests to gods who were not pleased with his decisions. More than that, they were sure that Sone Dedthanou himself carried within him agents of evil, unkind spirits.

His mother was something of a medium, a woman who would and could, at times, suddenly become "spirit-filled," who could dance in what appeared to be trances, and who could, in certain moments, trustingly predict future events. Being a medium to the spirit world was, in fact, her profession, her life's work, he says. She made money because people were confident that she could tell them what was going to happen in their lives.

An odd parental mix, really: on one side, his father, a sincere unbeliever, a man whose deep faith in the supernatural led him to distrust any single religion or faith; and on the other, his mother, something of a charlatan, he says, a liar, a woman who manipulated the hopes and fears of those who came to her with money in their hands for a vision he has since come to believe that she created out of her own vivid imagination. She was, he says a bit derisively, something of a "performer."

If we want to know how it was that Deuane Ksopsmopsou remembered Sone Dedthanou in Thailand as a ruthless thug, we need to keep in mind the significance of spirituality in the home in which he was raised and the undeniable effects that his parents, like all parents, had on him, because Sone Dedthanou was not simply a thug.

School in Laos

His father wanted more for him than the military in his native Thailand, so, at thirteen years old, Sone Dedthanou moved across the Mekong River to Laos, where one of his older sisters already lived. If he went to Laos, he could get more education, his father reasoned, and his father noticed something about this particular child — his fifth of twelve. Sone was a smart boy who needed school, a good education that he could receive only in Laos.

So Sone spent the next several years in schools across the Mekong River. At eighteen, even though his father had sent him to Laos to avoid the military service, he joined the army of General Kolang, the political middle of the three factions fighting for control of Laos. Sone was, he says, most comfortable with the forces in the political center, and it was as clear to him as it was to others that the best life available at the time was the military.

Because of his education, he started working as a nurse in a hospital when General Kolang's people were banished to the middle of the Laotian countryside.

But when fighting resumed again, Sone Dedthanou found himself in a difficult world of unjustifiable opposites. Sometimes he was a killer, a murderer. When you fight, he says, you *will* be killed, after all, if you don't kill first. On other days, he was a healer, a preserver of the very precious gift of life he had taken with no remorse just a day before.

He was nineteen years old and very confused about good and evil. He'd come from a home of religious and spiritual contradictions and entered a world of irreconcilable opposites. But like his father, he says, he never quite lost his desire to find real spiritual truth. "I was always looking for a true God," he'll tell you today. "What I didn't know was where I was."

Geographically back then, he lived in small town just south of Vientiane. For a time, even though peace ruled, peace found no place in his soul. When he continued to practice something of the medicine he'd learned as an army nurse, his ability to heal became his identity and his calling card. People called him "the doctor" because he dispensed medicine and brought healing that some felt was miraculous.

One man came to him because his mouth was twisted from what Sone thinks may have been a mild stroke. He dispensed some medicine and soon enough, perhaps as much by time as anything, the man's face straightened out. People believed that the man's mouth was misshapen because of an evil spirit; to see that same man without the vestiges that spirit had left made those same people feel that Sone was a spiritual cleanser, and that reputation only increased his perceived power. In fact, some people came to believe that they would be healed even before he saw them. He seemed a miracle worker. He seemed, in some ways, as magical as his mother. He seemed almost a god.

He met his wife, Seng, when she came to him for treatment. He was twenty-nine when he married her, and the town was thrilled by their courtship and their marriage. He was, after all, a miracle worker.

A different Sone

At night, however, a different character emerged. The healer became an avenger, a man given to violence and double-dealing, his lair none other than Buddhist temples in the region. In most villages, the local temple was also a community center.

When priests needed money, they rented out space to almost any kind of revelry, turning the temple into a mini–Las Vegas. Booze, drugs, gambling, prostitution—the full range of social ills that compound most every society found a base of operations, for a time, in the local temple. Legitimate and illegitimate businesses secured their own corners as the place became a sordid county fair, rife with graft, corruption, and all forms of immorality.

He seemed a miracle worker . . . . He seemed almost a god.

Who wielded power in such a bazaar? The thugs, the tough guys, the big men capable of strong-arming the others into bribes and payoffs. They were bouncers of sorts, but much worse—double-dealers who were themselves involved in every vice available on-site. And who led the thugs? You guessed it: Sone Dedthanou.

By day, he was dispensing health and even playing a kind of god. By night, he was the godfather of thugs, keeping order in an event that was one part community celebration, another part brothel and gambling den.

And all during this time, he'll tell you, he was looking hard for peace, personal peace. If you think that's incongruent, think of Ecclesiastes. Really, there's nothing new under the sun, wherever that sun rises or sets.

When the communists took over Laos in 1975, their own brand of Puritanism ended the temple debauchery by which Sone had become both strong and wealthy. After two months in an indoctrination camp, he told the communists that he was mending his ways and going back to his family and a plot of land where they could grow some rice. Meanwhile, his wife had complained that, with her husband in the internment camp, there was no one to provide for the family. When he came home, there was nothing, and for the first time in his life, Sone Dedthanou felt hunger eating away at body and soul.

For the next fifteen years, his family growing quickly, he tried every possible scheme to provide for them. Perhaps that's too kind a description—for the next fifteen years, Sone Dedthanou did everything he could to make money.

Moving up

For a time, in Thailand, he worked for a politician, a man with lots of clout, but he will readily admit that inside his heart and soul Sone Dedthanou hadn't changed much at all. His sin had become more respectable; he'd moved from blue-collar to white-collar crime. Wine, women, and song went out with his new political standing, but corruption and graft quickly moved in, filling his soul's empty dark corners. Given his prominence and high standing, people now thought of him as a winner, he says, but "I knew I was a winner only because I knew how to play the game." He may well have been less of a thug, but he was no less—and maybe even more—of a crook.

Still, life wasn't easy. His family now included six children, and there was not a lot of money. It may be difficult to see how a corrupt politician can be needy, but think of it this way: if a man comes to a politician with a bribe to get himself free from the law's reach, that politician needs to spend a significant amount of that cash to buy off the judge. Thus, even though there's money everywhere, little ends up in his pocket.

Even though he was never far from power and authority, Sone was not happy with his life or his fortune, so he decided to take his whole family to a Lao refugee camp and try to get to America, something new.

Starting over new again

A year passed, including several months training in the English language. Finally, a sponsor was located, a Presbyterian minister in Houston, Texas, and Sone and his family left for the United States.

In that Presbyterian church in Houston, some ancient memory returned through the music. Once again, just as when he was a little boy listening to the guitar strings of the motorcycle evangelist, Sone Dedthanou found himself trying to sing along with music he didn't know and words that, to him, only faintly resembled human language. What he remembers about that church was how strange it felt to try to give words to ideas that had no meaning. "I knew there was something in those words," he says today, "but I didn't know what they meant."

What the searcher did find, however, was the outside chance that there was, here in this new faith, another source for truth, the real truth that he, like his father, had always been looking for. When he would sing the words of those songs, he says, he'd tell himself that "maybe this is the truth."

Through other Laotian people, Sone discovered that there was work in a place called South Sioux City, Nebraska. He obtained permission from his sponsor to leave his family behind in Texas while he went in search of a good job, then left, eight months after arriving in America. He lived in Nebraska for little more than a month before discovering that an old acquaintance, a man named Deuane Ksopsmopsou, was living and working in a town even farther north, a town named Worthington, Minnesota.

After the trip up north to cold Minnesota, Sone says, Ron Lammers's car simply gave up— "it couldn't go any farther."

It was Deuane who told him about this American man who could speak Laotian, a preacher named Ron Lammers, and it was Ron Lammers who told Sone that he could move his entire family up north from Texas to live in Worthington, where Sone could study English and at least have a chance at getting along in this new culture.

That was early winter, 1984, and it was a long trip back to Minnesota from Houston, eight people in one car. Sone's oldest child was fifteen, the youngest, just three. After the trip up north to cold Minnesota, Sone says, Ron Lammers's car simply gave up—"it couldn't go any farther."

Not by wish but still by obligation, Sone Dedthanou began to attend yet another Christian church; after all, it had been a preacher who'd sponsored him originally and yet another preacher who'd gone out of his way to haul his entire family up north from Texas. But the only element of worship that connected at all with him was music, the faint stirrings of one long-ago childhood afternoon in Thailand and the recent reminiscence of music sung in a church in Texas, music that made him wonder whether there was something honestly worth seeking in the way these American people came together in their temples.

At that time, Khay Baccam was preaching in the Lao language once a month in Worthington, and the worship was a kind of gathering of Lao people. Sone went, not because he thought that he'd be converted but because his people were there, his children's friends. And that's when something remarkable happened, something incredible, something that his old friend Deuane Ksopsmopsou absolutely couldn't believe.

The Christian God in the Lao language

When he heard the will of God in the Lao language, Sone says, he remembered what had happened when he was a boy and he remembered what had gone on in that Presbyterian church in Houston, even though he'd not, back then, seemed particularly interested.

All of that came back to him vividly, he says, and something in him — some kind of tracking instinct maybe — prompted him to weave together a single story by its remnant threads.

This is the way he describes what happened within himself: "I started to think that maybe God had a plan for me. I started to think that maybe I had to study about this thing called Christianity."

And when he studied the Bible with Khay and others, when he took the time to read what he could about Jesus Christ, he came to understand something about the questions that had haunted him his entire life, even in those times that he was as far from righteous as a human being could ever be. "I came to understand that this Jesus was the Messiah," he says. He came to see that this Savior was what he was looking for throughout all of those years.

The gospel of John, Chapter 4, he says, prompted something miraculous, a sea change in his whole way of looking at himself and his world. It was the story of Jesus and the Samaritan woman at the well. Christ asks the woman to get water for him. She says, "You are a Jew—how is it you speak to a Samaritan? After all, you know who I am." Jesus then tells her about the living water he can draw, the water that will leave her thirst-less. He tells her about herself, her sin, her five husbands. And then she says that he must be a prophet because he knows so very much. She tells him that her forefathers worshiped in the mountains, but she says that she's confused about what the Jews are saying—that they must now worship in Jerusalem.

... when he took the time to read what he could about Jesus Christ, he came to understand something about the questions that had haunted him his entire life, even in those times that he was as far from righteous as a human being could ever be.

That's when Jesus tells her that a time is coming "and has now come when the true worshipers will worship the Father in spirit and in truth."

"I know that Messiah is coming," the Samaritan woman says, joyfully, "and then he will explain everything to us."

Then the same words that filled her with faith flashed like nothing less than eternal truth through the eyes and into the heart and soul of Sone Dedthanou. "I who speak to you," Jesus tells the Samaritan woman, "am he."

Jesus is the Messiah. Jesus is the one she has been seeking. Jesus Christ is the truth Sone Dedthanou had been seeking through all those years in Laos, in Thailand, and in the short time he and his family had lived in the United States.

Conviction. Almost immediately, he went home and talked to his wife and children. "I think I know the Messiah," he told them. "Do you love me?"

They said, "Yes, of course we do."

"Then we have to go together," Sone told them all. "We have to follow Jesus Christ—the whole family, from now on."

Somehow, Sone Dedthanou had found himself ministered to, as if he were—this ex-thug—the Samaritan woman at the well, as if he'd been sitting there listening to the Savior tell him personally that, yes, he was the Savior, the Messiah.

Through his whole life, Sone Dedthanou had prayed; he'd prayed without ceasing. But until he sat there at the well one day, the Samaritan woman beside him, until he'd heard with his own ears in his own language that this Jesus Christ was the Messiah that both of them—that woman and he—had forever been searching for, until that moment the prayers were offered only to a mysterious spiritual something. From the day he found the Messiah, he prayed to a Someone who was, to him, as real as the man at the well. He decided to follow Jesus Christ, and he was baptized on September 14, 1991.

Nine years later, after years of Bible studies and training, after numerous conferences of Lao Christians and boot camp training for leadership, after growing in the Christian faith, Sone Dedthanou, once a thug, once a crook, became a leader for the Lord. He was ordained as pastor of the Worthington Lao church.

"God's place in my life means more than I can say," he'll tell you today. "He lived in me when I was a small boy, only eight years old. He lived in me throughout my life in Laos. He lived in me even when I did many bad things."

Is his life now without difficulties? Of course not. Whose is? "Even right now," he says, "when I have problems, I still have peace."

Because of all he's been through himself, because of all of the sin he's seen and committed himself through a long lifetime on two continents, he can pass peace to others very easily. "If people talk about gangs and get worried about their children, I tell them that I don't worry — I've been there already. I know what it is like. I can see very clearly that God has been leading me through all of that, and for that reason," he says, "I will give my life to him. I will go right on serving him."

Pastor Sone Dedthanou's story is the testimony of someone saved by grace, truly amazing grace.

PAHN ARNOULUC

Subsistence

It's simple enough to say it—Pahn Arnouluc was born in 1972, the oldest son of his parents, in Sayyaboulee, Laos, a small community on the country's western edge, between the Thai border and the Mekong River. His parents, like almost everyone in the village and its neighborhood, were farmers— subsistence farmers. All of that is simple enough.

No single fact of his personal history, however, is more important to understanding where Pahn is today than the fact that at the time of his birth, his father was fighting *for* American interests and *with* the invading South Vietnamese troops, in an expansion of the Vietnam War—west into Laos.

The invading South Vietnamese troops attempted to break the North Vietnamese supply route, the Ho Chi Minh Trail. A collateral effect of the operation, however, was to drive the Lao communist forces, the Pathet Lao, deeper into Laos, extending hostilities into a country that had only precariously maintained its own peace since the departure of the colonial

French in the early 1950s.

In America, antiwar protests became more frequent and more violent both on and off university campuses. But the bearded and beaded weren't the only war protestors anymore. By 1972, the year Pahn was born, the list of politicians and celebrities who began questioning the war had grown long. Support for the war effort waned quickly; the only returns from the significant military effort seemed to be fifty thousand-plus American soldiers in body bags.

As Americans grew weary, the government offered enormous military and economic aid to Laos, financing over twenty thousand Thai troops so they could cross the border and help take on the communist Pathet Lao forces. Among those twenty thousand was Pahn Arnouluc's father.

Throughout Laos, fighting persisted, heavy fighting, until February of 1973, when Pahn was a year old and the Laotian cease-fire was declared in Paris, just a few weeks after the United States and North Vietnamese twenty-five-article peace accords. That treaty spelled out the end of American military involvement and was described by President Richard Nixon as a compromise that offered "peace with honor."

The last American combat soldiers left Southeast Asia a month later, in March 1973, although some military advisors and Marines who were protecting U.S. installations remained until 1975. At just about that time, Pathet Lao forces took control of Laos and abolished the monarchy.

"Peace with honor" was an attempt to offer some political cover so American troops could leave Southeast Asia, but it did not prevent carnage throughout the region in the aftermath of that withdrawal. In the next twenty years, according to some estimates, over three hundred thousand were simply murdered by the communist Pathet Lao, including the royal family, former government officials, military personnel, generals, their associates and family members.

If Americans have any lingual reference to this time, it is what they associate with one horrific phrase: "the killing fields." What followed was murder—massacres, in fact—

chemical bombings, tortures, genocide. And what followed the killing fields was the creation of Lao refugee camps in Thailand to deal with an immense refugee crisis.

A child of war

Pahn Arnouluc is too young to remember any of that. His mother told him about the day the Pathet Lao came to Sayyaboulee to arrest the soldiers from town and send them all to Champasak, a "re-education" or "seminar" camp located far to the south, seemingly a world away. Among those arrested and dispatched was his father. Although Pahn himself doesn't remember that day, it was the last time he ever saw him.

With her husband gone, more than a day's travel away in a prison camp, Pahn's mother, full of fear, took it upon herself to leave the village where she'd been born and her own family had lived for as long as she could remember. What she feared was no illusion: at any time, the communist forces could return and simply take the families of those men who had fought against the Pathet Lao. Her own parents had already left the village, fearing retribution. Their leaving was, to her—and to the entire family—not merely a strategy, but a matter of life or death.

Every member of the first generation of Lao immigrants to this country has an escape story, but Pahn was only a child when he and his mother left Laos; his memories are no less intense than many of those who were older, but they are more fragmentary: his mother shaking him awake in the middle of the night; the firm hold of his grandfather's hand on his own; the soggy darkness of the jungle, a place, as a child, he'd always feared; the concern written in his mother's eyes; the black night's palpable silence; his little sister's innocence; the furtive warnings not to cry, not to make a noise; a fearsome enemy skulking in the darkness all around; the hush—as if no one on earth should know they were leaving; the rain all night—everything soaked; hiding out all day long in the jungle; the seamlessness of night and day.

He and his family were not caught. They weren't seen by anyone who reported them. Unlike that of so many others, Pahn's story of escape to Thailand is not about acute suffering or death and dying. They didn't cross the Mekong River, because they crossed the border where there is no Mekong. Pahn's grandfather knew the way because he'd taken it before, more than once. Across the border in Thailand, they were greeted sympathetically, both by strangers and by some old friends who'd already escaped, like them, now refugees.

They were free, free at least from the danger of death or immediate deportation. They were free to speak openly, free to be seen. But they were not free from care.

The word *subsist* has a very simple meaning—"to continue to exist." To people like Pahn, the word has meaning that contemporary America finds nearly impossible to imagine. He was a child, five or six years old. Once in Thailand, he didn't go to school because there was no school. Even if there had been, he would not have attended because the new free life in Thailand required *subsistence* living, a way of life based upon the most basic human need, the need simply to exist.

This was the regimen of *subsistence:* get up early, go into the jungle, see what you can find—animals, fruit, medicinal herbs—and bring back whatever you can, if not to eat, to sell, often to the only people who had money to buy, the soldiers.

This was the regimen of *subsistence:* get up early, go into the jungle, see what you can find—animals, fruit, medicinal herbs—and bring back whatever you can, if not to eat, to sell, often to the only people who had money to buy, the soldiers.

His mother worked in the same way, while waiting to hear something, anything, about her husband. Occasionally, a relative or friend who had also left Laos would venture back across the border to see if anyone had heard anything at all of her husband—he'd been taken south to a camp—"you remember him? Has anyone seen him?" But there was nothing.

Her husband's return wasn't out of the question, however. Some men did come back; some escaped the concentration camps. Whenever someone would return, Pahn's family would ask about his father. Nothing.

Many never did come back from those camps though, because horrible things happened there, and everyone knew it.

Ten years after crossing the border into Thailand, Pahn, now eighteen years old, lugging whatever plunder he could take from the jungle, would occasionally walk four or five hours to the city, where the sales were always far better. But the city, despite its possibilities, held other problems. He was, after all, a Lao boy in Thailand, and he was undocumented. Without proper identification, he was limited in what jobs he could take because he was an "illegal," a man—a boy—without a green card. His only way of life was to keep moving, picking up jobs wherever he could, often in places where his employment was part of the black market.

He was eating, at least, and in Thailand neither he nor anyone else in his family was in danger of being discovered by the Pathet Lao. But life on the run wasn't easy; he was always worried about being caught for being illegal. When after two years away from his mother and her new husband—she had needed a man, a provider, to care for her and her children— he returned to that Thai village full of Lao immigrants, the decision was made to enroll in a refugee camp.

Pahn Arnouluc didn't make that decision himself, and he certainly wasn't the only one to leave. When United Nations workers came to pick them up and take them away, he and his extended family, along with about a hundred others, were ready to go. A bus came to get them.

Leaving

By then, the United Nations refugee workers were very interested in helping—it was 1988. Laotian refugees in Thailand continued to be a problem, not only in sheer numbers, but also because of the ecological damage being done to the Southeast Asian rain forests by thousands of people just like Pahn ransacking the jungle.

What motivated them—Pahn and his mother and his step-father and all of the others who'd decided to leave en masse—was the hope that such a move would create a better life. By 1988, thousands of Lao refugees had already left for America, for Australia, for Canada, and elsewhere. By that time, news of places where life was easier had filtered back to the many people still living in Thai camps. When almost one hundred people climbed on those U.N. buses that day in 1988, what prompted their enthusiasm was the conviction that subsistence was not the best they could do for themselves and their families. Somewhere else, there had to be a better way to live.

Young and handsome, Pahn was given a job as a guard in that first refugee camp. It was his job to sit on the quarreling and quell the fighting when it broke loose, to shut off the camp lights once it was time for everyone to sleep. It was a wonderful job, he says, not simply because of the authority, but because it offered him access to more food than he'd ever had.

In America today, it may be almost impossible to think of eating as a necessity, not a form of recreation. It is. Even when there is no food, people must eat. Today, Pahn is thirty-two years old, clean-cut, handsome, healthy; it is difficult to imagine him as physically needy. But what he remembers best about his first legitimate job, a job in a refugee camp in Thailand, was that it got him food. He'd gone up a step or two from subsistence living.

That first camp was a temporary holding compound, not structured to prepare refugees for immigration and a new life in a new culture. The next camp was dedicated specifically to those who wanted to go to the United States of America. There, for the most part, his days were filled with studying—language, customs, and behavior that more than occasionally seemed incredible, even ridiculous. He worked as a kind of nurse's assistant in that camp, a good job, he says. He remembers having to clean up hospital rooms, removing dead bodies when necessary, then bringing in the next round of patients.

Pahn first heard about Jesus Christ in the United Nations refugee camp, first heard a gospel he didn't begin to understand back then; he admits that readily. What he learned there was that this God had something to do with the concept of ownership. "Who owns the world?" some Christian evangelist asked him and others. "Everything in this life has an owner, but you tell me who it is that *owns* the whole world?"

It seemed to him — then and now — to be an intriguing question. Whether he believed anything at all about gods or religion was also a good question, he admits; but it seemed very clear to him that there were good reasons to hang out with the Christians. The church offered cookies and other goodies, not to mention clothes, good clothes. You could walk into a religious place like that and pick up a brand-new shirt for nothing at all — not bad for someone whose only way of life had been *subsistence*.

"Who owns the world?" some Christian evangelist asked him and others. "Everything in this life has an owner, but you tell me who it is that *owns* the whole world?"

Besides, it was rumored that the Christians had special powers; they could make things happen faster, facilitate a family's leaving for the States. Having to listen to somebody talk about who owned the world was not too great a price for a new jacket or shirt or a quicker trip to California.

Besides, everyone knew that the United States wasn't a Buddhist nation — it was a Christian nation. If you wanted to know more about this place, it was a good idea to listen to someone go on and on about this God, the owner, the one who claimed, oddly enough, to be the only true God, and this Son of his who died so sadly and then rose again, this Jesus. It was an interesting story.

Once he could tell it himself, once he could reorganize

the words the Christian man had said and offer them back to him, just a few months before he came to America, Pahn was, in that camp, baptized into the Christian faith. "I was a Christian," he says today, "but not much of one." And then he laughs.

But it's not a scornful laugh. It's hardly a laugh at all. That laugh is maybe a step-and-a-half more than a smile, but lively enough to kick up a few staggered breaths. The first time you meet Pahn Arnouluc, you'll see very quickly that he seems very happy. His smile is, in fact, part of his charming good looks, the kind of face you might see on billboards or television. If you'd look at a lineup of recent immigrants, you'd likely pick out Pahn as one who could easily make it in America—there's charm in his face and eyes.

Among those who know him best in Sioux City's Lao Unity Church, few have immigrant stories that are easier to tell. Most people remember more suffering. He and his family got wet on their escape into Thailand, but their suffering barely tips the balance when compared with so many other refugee families.

Most of his life before immigrating was literally hand-to-mouth, subsistence living; but then, whose wasn't? And by the time he and his family finally arrived in California, in 1988, there was already an established Lao community to help him through the misadventures and mishaps that all immigrants fall into.

Of all of his friends and fellow believers at church and in the community, Pahn Arnouluc— handsome Pahn Arnouluc—may seem, well, most American, most unsullied by suffering, untouched by the painful remnant memories of the Lao killing fields.

California

In 1990, Pahn and his family left Bangkok and flew to San Francisco, where relatives already there had paved the way for them. They picked up his family from the airport and drove them right to Fresno, where his sponsor, his cousin, already had a place for all of them.

It didn't take long to find a job at a Chinese restaurant, where he could work during those hours when he wasn't going to school. "Right away," he says, "it was wonderful to be here."

"I still made a lot of mistakes," he says, demonstrating with his hands. "I don't know how to open a can. I don't know how to open sauce," he says, and he laughs as he fumbles through a demonstration.

But if awkward fingers on strange kitchen tools were almost the extent of his difficulties adjusting to life in America, then Pahn had it easier than most.

In 1991, some Laotian people came to California and told the community that good money could be made in a place named Kansas—Garden City, Kansas. "Cut meat," they said. "Come to Kansas and cut meat." So Pahn did and worked at an IBP (Iowa Beef Processors) plant there for a year before his stepfather got sick and his family needed him back in Fresno.

But there was no work in California—and little income, so when his stepfather slowly regained strength, Pahn decided to head back to the Midwest. When the Garden City IBP plant told him they had no immediate openings, he ended up in Des Moines, Iowa, where a man named Somsak, a man who helped the Lao people get their feet on the ground, gave him the phone number of a place in Sioux City, Iowa, where another IBP plant was looking for more meat cutters.

Almost immediately, Pahn drove his car west to Sioux City, asked for a job, and was hired on the spot. Since he had no place to live, that night he slept in his car in the IBP parking lot.

That was September of 1993, and he's been there ever since—thirteen years now, cutting meat and sometimes working in packaging, since IBP allows people to move around in the business if they'd like. It's a good job, and he likes it, a reason for joy.

For the most part, he stayed with the church, although

there were times—that year in Garden City, for example—when he didn't associate at all with Christian believers. Back in Fresno, accompanied by their sponsor, his parents were going to church frequently; but always there were ulterior motives—an unending source of help negotiating the terrain of a brand-new culture, not to mention food, clothing, relief. Christians did things for people. An hour or two in a worship service they understood little of was well worth such wide and lucrative benefits.

That he came to Sioux City alone did not mean, of course, that he stayed alone. IBP had dozens of Laotian workers, and Sioux City was full of established Southeast Asian immigrants. Each day at the factory, he worked alongside those who spoke his language, had similar memories, laughed at the same jokes, ate the same foods.

One of those was Dokmai Vongphakdy, who talked Pahn into coming along to church in Sioux City, to a Lutheran fellowship that had attracted many others from the Lao community. It was Dokmai who lined him up with a roommate so that his living expenses wouldn't drain most of what he earned at the factory. It was Dokmai who had a daughter. And it was Dokmai who invited him, after a time, to move in with the family, to move in with her daughter.

And it's not hard to understand why. Pahn had already established himself as a hard worker, maintaining steady employment at the plant. Pahn had come along to church for quite some time, even though he admits today that his level of faith during those months and years wasn't much different than it had been after his first exposure to the Christian faith in the camp.

Pahn's bright and engaging smile would prompt almost any mother to find him a more than suitable candidate for an eligible daughter. The relationship wasn't exactly engineered, but it was, certainly, artfully designed.

A year after he moved in with her, they were married. In a few years there were children, two of them, Tukhata and Nina.

Then, suddenly, his wife left him and moved in with someone else. Just as suddenly, Pahn was alone, far more alone than he'd been in his entire life.

Pahn's story may well begin in a time long before he drew breath, a time when his father fought a war in the jungles of Laos for an ideology that didn't win. In his first sixteen years in Laos and Thailand, subsistence was simply a way of life. Even today, fifteen years or more after immigration, the English language is something of a problem for him. Pahn Arnouluc, despite his successes at IBP, his vigilant church-going, his car, his relative wealth, his wonderful laugh, is still very much a hyphenated American, an immigrant.

But the burden he carries today isn't really part of the traditional immigrant package. Separation, divorce, the breaking of vows is something that happens far too often around all of us today, regardless of ethnic character, of socioeconomic level, and even, pitiably, of well-meant professions of faith. No community has escaped the suffering caused by the breakdown of family life.

Pahn Arnouluc's most profound problem today is more uniquely American than it is Thai or Somalian or Mexican. Divorce happens as frequently in modern suburbia as it does in any of this country's hyphenated communities.

Right now, Pahn feels the grip of a sadness that really never quite passes. He's been able to see Tukhata and Nina more often lately, and that's a great help. But he's been left for another, and that rejection—and his isolation—is not easy.

And yet, he smiles. If you would see him today, on the job or at church, you would never guess that he is alone.

And he isn't.

"I have God in my heart to help me," he says today. And what he knows today — after many hours of study and prayer and counseling — is that the Bible tells him what's going on in his life. It's God Almighty — and Jesus his Son — that brings him his joy.

How? Forgiveness. He says he's learned something he'd never even heard of before becoming a Christian believer — forgiveness. He can see her now, with the other man, and his heart is not choked with self-pity or hate, because he's learned to work at forgiveness. "That is difficult to understand for someone who doesn't know God," he says, with the confident smile of one who does.

Today, Pahn and Dokmai, his mother-in-law, the woman who first took him to church, are very close. They are one, he says, and they are happy. They wish what happened didn't happen, but they are united in their love for the children, in their desire to forgive, in the love they have for Jesus Christ.

Really, you might say, Pahn Arnouluc knows today more than ever that he is not alone.

His father

And then this. Not long ago, Pahn heard from an uncle that his father — his birth father — was still alive. After all of those years, a quarter century and more, someone heard from him. He's still in the camp where he was taken all of those years ago, but today his father is free to go, if he would like.

When he heard that news, Pahn wrote to his father, in care of the camp. Soon enough, his father wrote him back. And then he called his father, called him from Sioux City, Iowa, all the way back to a camp in southern Laos, and the two of them — almost as if for the first time — spoke together. It was, he says, a blessing for both of them.

Back when he claims he didn't know much at all about the

Christian faith, back when he was baptized in that first Thai refugee camp, he says what he remembers learning is that God is, in fact, the owner of everything. He owns what's on high and what's below, Pahn says, and his own hope, in life and in death, in light and in darkness, is with that God.

For most of his boyhood in Thailand, Pahn Arnouluc lived, from hand to mouth, you might say, a subsistence living, a life based on finding enough simply to stay alive, finding enough food to sustain himself.

Today, even in his sadness, he knows he has enough food for all of his needs. Today, he has the bread of life.

KONGKHAM
SAENGTHAMMAVONG

In Strength and Weakness

When Kongkham Saengthammavong and his wife Vieng stood on the banks of the Mekong River, ready to attempt an escape, they were convinced that the decision to cross over, no matter how dangerous, was the right thing to do, their only option. With them was their son, their only child, Kai, five years old at the time; their only means of conveyance across the river, a single banana tree.

They were convinced that their future, and their son's, was somewhere other than Laos, somewhere else in the world. "My wife and I—we talked together," he remembers. "We told each other that we had no future in Laos." The Pathet Lao takeover had occurred four years earlier, and Kong had spent two long years in a prison camp, where the new regime attempted to get him and many, many others reeducated in the new system.

But it wasn't the prison camp experience that convinced them, and it wasn't the fact that he'd nearly wasted away, starved at the hands of those he'd once considered his enemies. Instead, it was the kind of life they were leading in so-called freedom, a hand-to-mouth existence of buying and selling, buying and selling, day in, day out, in a world where there were simply no other options. The only way to make a living was to buy more and sell cheaper in a frantic pace at the daily market. Life offered no promise.

That communist snipers regularly shot refugees right out of the Mekong was a given. Everyone knew that. They had come alone to the river, confident a smaller party would draw less attention.

"I was not scared," Kongkham will tell you with every bit of the force of his considerable character. "I was not scared."

The weight of his commitment to escape pushed both of them—him and his wife—into commitment. That's why he wasn't afraid. He was determined—they both were. They were going to cross the Mekong. They were absolute in their conviction. There was nothing for them in Laos. They were going to escape, and there was no room in their dedication for fear.

But the strength of their commitment had another source, and Kongkham Saengthammavong explains it this way—there was, for them, very little to separate life from death. In a moment, in the flash of a rifle from shore, you could be dead. Just as easily, if you had the rifle in your hands yourself, he'll tell you, you would kill whoever tried to stop you. The sheer proximity of violent death on a daily basis created a desperate fatalism that's unlike anything, or so it seems, in American culture. "If you die, you die," he explains, with a coldness that seems, even to him, so very matter-of-fact.

Even today, Kongkham Saengthammavong is a man of clear and decisive resolution. When he tells his story, he explains things as though he were teaching, his eyes deeply set, eyebrows arched. Life itself is a serious business. He can and will turn a quick smile and laugh robustly, and he doesn't seem stern. Ask him to see the pictures of his family, and he'll beam as widely as any proud grandfather. But what is central to understanding him is his resilient strength, his resolve.

That's why it's important to see him—and his wife and their son—there on the banks of the Mekong. It's dark, and in his arm there's that single banana tree they will swim beside to make their way across the river. The Mekong flows slowly, methodically. The Missouri River, just a bit north from where he lives today in South Sioux City, Nebraska, flows much, much faster.

What drove both him and Vieng that night—and still drives them—is a sheer force of will. Kongkham believes in human action. That belief— that all of us need to take control of our lives—is why they were so convinced that the escape was worth the terrifying risks.

That belief—that all of us need to take control of our lives—is why they were so convinced that the escape was worth the terrifying risks.

They made it, obviously. With one arm around that tree, the other hand on his son, and Vieng holding on behind, the three of them— they all were swimmers—slowly paddled and paddled their way across the water to freedom. No shots rang out, no blood flowed that night.

Today, they live a world away. Kongkham and Vieng both cut meat at Tyson's, a meat-packing plant, as they have ever since they came to Siouxland. Kai, their son, now twenty-seven years old, works with computers at Security National Bank, Sioux City.

It's their deep-seated resolve that mattered that night, their determination to improve their lives at all costs—that characteristic is of greatest importance in plotting the story of Kong's life. His strength is crucial to an understanding of where he is—and they are—today, an unlikely place perhaps, for a determined man like Kong. Together, he and Vieng are under God's wings.

Schoolboy

Kongkham's life begins in Vientiane, the capital of Laos, where his father was a soldier. Disciplined, authoritative, exacting, Kong's father had very clear plans for his eight children and was decisive in carrying them out. "My father — very strict," Kong says, laughing, almost as if it is safe to say so now, with the insulation of so many years. For each of them, Kong's father wanted an education — it was something he insisted upon. For Kong, the second, that meant years of schooling, nine in fact, an education that makes him somewhat unique among this region's refugees.

While strict fathers do not always create respect, Kong's father did because no matter how successful he was militarily, he always cared for his family, providing well. Kong himself would be nearly thirty before he knew deprivation, poverty, and hunger. His was a very good Laotian childhood, and education was free to those who could, after all, afford the luxury. His family was, in American terms, middle-class, not peasant farmers. It was his extensive education — and the socioeconomic level at which he lived — that secured him the job that would determine much of the course of his life in Laos.

Laotian Army MP

In 1970, at the age of nineteen, Kong entered the military, perhaps the most promising profession for men like him at the time, no matter what their political allegiance. There, because of his education and his standing in Laotian society, he quickly found a place among the military police. But to be an MP in Laos between 1962, when a final attempt at coalition government failed, and 1975, when the communist-backed Pathet Lao finally took total control of the country, requires some explanation.

For most of that time, the country was in various stages of chaos — coups and countercoups and nearly constant civil war. What's more, the entire populace had become participants in the Vietnam War, often pawns to superpowers warring throughout Southeast Asia. Thai mercenaries were fighting for the Royal Lao government, CIA-backed tribesmen operated under the direction of the United States and its allies, and the Pathet Lao were financed by the Chinese and the Russians. Laos was drawn and quartered by competing military forces. During the years Kong was in the army, Laos was anything but unified.

In the middle of such chaos, authority inevitably is in the hands of the military. Where an army is the de facto government, the military police determines the definitions of justice; they have the biggest guns. Most Americans might think of an MP as someone whose jurisdiction ends at the gates of the military post; in Laos, however, during the years Kong was in the military, an MP's authority extended into civilian neighborhoods as well. Put bluntly, an MP answered to no one, except commanding officers, when they were around. An MP enforced the law that he and his cohorts created.

During this time, Kong admits that he was, in his own words, a "mean dude." War was raging all around; more than occasionally he'd be a part of it, on the front lines. But when he wasn't, he was an investigator, an interrogator, an enforcer, a man whose job it was to determine truth, guilt, and innocence in any way he saw fit—and then sentence accordingly. Things happened back then that weren't pretty and may well be best forgotten.

When he tells you today—and he will—that at one time, back there in his homeland, he had visions of becoming a lawyer, those visions arose because during those years he operated as a lawyer does—*and* as a judge. *He* determined who was right and who was wrong, *he* redressed injustice, *he* punished the guilty. *He* was the law—and he liked that, in part because he liked order and regulation. Even today, his friends will tell you, in the Lao Unity Church where he is a member, he likes to have things organized. Kong likes things to run well.

A chance meeting

Fast forward quickly, almost twenty-five years. Kongkham Saengthammavong is buying groceries in a store in South Sioux City, Nebraska. Out front of him is a shopping cart, maybe a quarter full. Slowly, he's walking down an aisle.

When he looks up, he sees a strangely familiar face, a face he recognizes from those years, the early 1970s, in Laos, the years before the Pathet Lao takeover. He's not sure, of course, because so many years have passed and it seems so impossible that he might run into that man—in the middle of this huge country.

The man who is coming his way also believes that the man shopping in front of him isn't really a stranger. Both think that they know each other; neither is sure of why or who the other is. Just before their grocery carts nearly collide, they speak—in the Laotian language—and soon enough, in just a few seconds, they remember everything.

The man Kong met in the grocery store that day was Khay Baccam, and the two of them *did* know each other a quarter century ago in Laos, not because Khay was in the military but because he was an arms smuggler making good money by operating beyond the limits of whatever law existed. He was wealthy enough to be able to buy immunity; his money created safety for his black marketeering. He knew people like Kong, powerful MPs, because in his line of work he had to deal with them every day. Kongkham Saengthammavong *was* the law, what there was of it, and big players like Khay needed to know whose palms required grease. If that scenario smells like corruption, it was; but then most of us didn't live in Laos during those turbulent final years of the Vietnam War. Vientiane was not, back then, South Sioux City.

At nineteen years old, educated, middle-class, son of a distinguished military captain, Kongkham slipped easily into the authority that came with being an MP. As disciplined, authoritative, and decisive as his father was, Kong grew to love the position he attained. He was in charge. He made the rules.

His strength was his will, his determination—and he wanted more.

Then came the communist takeover, however, and that power disappeared entirely. In 1975, anyone who had anything to do with authority in the old regime was immediately dragged off to prison camps—"seminars"—to be indoctrinated into the new way of life under the victorious Pathet Lao. Vieng stayed with her family in Vientiane. Kongkham Saengthammavong has memories of those days he doesn't care to review.

> **He was in charge. He made the rules. His strength was his will, his determination—and he wanted more.**

He left the prison camp two years later by arranging an escape with the driver of a delivery truck, someone he'd known from his days as an MP, a move that required untainted trust because the punishment for attempted escape was death on the spot. On his own, Kong secured passage out, and his escape was successful. He returned to Vientiane, to Vieng, where he became lost to the Pathet Lao, one of millions of city dwellers.

Freedom

Things could only improve, of course, and they did—his health returned, he was reunited with his family, and the walls that had surrounded his prison were gone. But life in Laos under the rule of the Pathet Lao was especially difficult for those not privileged by the communists, especially for those who, like Kong, had grown up middle-class and carried, at one time, significant power and standing.

Life, basically, was a daily flea market. Each day, thousands of people bought and sold or else, early in the morning, hiked out into the jungle to secure the goods they would try to peddle. No one was building nest eggs. There were no factory jobs. Survival depended totally on what you could barter or kill or steal.

That's why Kong and Vieng were united in their determination that, despite the dangers, they had to escape. Vieng's brother had already left and lived in a place called Niagara Falls. But even before he had left, he had written from Thailand and explained that they, too, should try to escape. The promises for the future were nil in Laos; if they were to live — in joy and prosperity — both of them knew that they would have to go to Thailand and leave Southeast Asia.

Not long after crossing the Mekong, Vieng and Kong were among the Laotian refugees at the camp at Nong Khai, then, a bit later, at Nakonphanom. At that time, 1979, most of them had been political prisoners in Laos; after 1981, many others followed, people who simply were seeking a better life.

Life in Thai refugee camps, he remembers, was really quite easy, especially when compared to life in Laos. Of food, there was plenty, and medical care was quite sufficient. In addition, camps created joyous reunions: many of those who made it out of Laos hadn't seen each other for years, prisoners of the Pathet Lao. To find each other again — alive — seemed a great blessing. Money flowed far more easily because many refugees had relatives who were already making money elsewhere in the world. Life at Nakonphanom wasn't a horror.

But he and Vieng, and their son, and now a daughter, Koung, left for the Philippines just sixteen months after arriving in Thailand. Many stayed longer, awaiting sponsorship and emigration. But many factors determined the pace at which people could be processed to leave. Among those were one's personal history. Because of Kong's position within the military police of the old regime, his case was dispatched quickly. Six months after leaving Thailand, and just less than two years after leaving Laos, he and Vieng and their two children landed in Niagara Falls, New York, where they were sponsored by a Roman Catholic church.

The transition to life in the United States was made far easier for them than it was for others because of Vieng's brother and his family, already settled in Niagara Falls, where her brother held a job in a grocery store. Kong's sponsors urged him not to find a job immediately, but instead to work hard at learning the language so as to increase his options. For a short time, he enrolled in a local middle school, where he was, by far, the oldest eighth grader. Meanwhile, his sponsors found Vieng a job.

It wouldn't be easy for any adult male to sit in a schoolroom beside students no older than his children, while his spouse was making a living. As prudent as his sponsor's advice may have been, for a man like Kong, who once had survived jungle warfare, wielded the authority of life and death, then endured prison camp and engineered his own escape, an American middle school was not a good fit.

With money Vieng had made, he bought an old Datsun for six hundred dollars (He'd learned to drive already in Laos) and headed for South Sioux City, Nebraska, where a brother claimed he could make good money in a packing plant. That was December 1986, and both he and Vieng had a job almost as soon as they arrived. They soon moved into a mobile home, where they lived for eleven years, until 1995, when they bought a house near the high school.

Kongkham's story is the kind of tale that anyone here in America would be proud of telling—how human initiative, the sheer will to succeed, has blossomed here in the land of opportunity.

Today, Kongkham Saengthammavong is most happy and proud to point out that all of his family members hold down jobs: he and Vieng are still employed by Tyson's; their son is at Security National Bank; their daughter Koung lives in Minneapolis, where she works as a receptionist; and their daughter, Noi, born in the States, is in telecommunication sales in Sioux City.

He has reason to be proud. Kongkham's story is the kind of tale that anyone here in America would be proud of telling—how human initiative, the sheer will to succeed, has blossomed here in the land of opportunity. Kongkham and Vieng's story is a single chapter from the book that is America — will, resolve, determination win here, after all. Their story is the very essence of the American dream.

A miracle

But little of that success matters, finally, to God Almighty, who, by his own testimony, tends to love us quite unconditionally, no matter what the peculiar force of our character. In fact, if his Word is to be believed, he'd rather tune his ear to the cries of those who come to him, not in strength but in weakness.

But then, there comes a time or two in almost all of our lives when even the strongest reach down and find no bootstraps to pull up. The Christian story, unlike the American dream, begins in weakness and ends in God's unconditional love, as does this one, the story of Kongkham and Vieng Saengthammavong.

One hot summer night in 2004, Kong got a frantic call from a close relative. Their son, Ali, just ten years old, suffered an asthma attack that wouldn't relent. An ambulance was called, and Ali was rushed off to Mercy Medical Center, where the family understood that the boy's predicament was very grave. Kong himself went to the hospital and watched in agonizing powerlessness. There was nothing they could do. Death seemed very near.

When Kong explains this chapter of his life's story, the manner of his telling shifts, as if what happened that night can only be understood in wonder — and, of course, in faith. At that moment, the man who describes himself at one time in his life as a "mean dude" had no decisive plan of action. The man who at another point in his life had taken on the administration of guilt and innocence to others, the man who'd engineered his escape from prison and his family's harrowing departure from Laos, stood by as if paralyzed, as did everyone else outside the boy's room.

Here's how he explains what happened. "I don't know why, but something tells me — 'oh, call Pastor Keo,'" even though

Kong didn't believe in the Christian God and never had, but considered himself a Buddhist, like his father. At times since his arrival in this country, he'd attended a Christian church to satisfy his sponsors, "but it meant nothing to me," he says. But something that night, in his powerlessness, told him to call his old friend Keo.

Keo Phommarath was someone he'd known for years. In and around Sioux City, they'd played together in a party band, Kong on keyboard, a band that had broken up when the members had become too busy. They hadn't been together for some time, but Kong knew that Keo had undergone some kind of change, that he'd become "Pastor Keo," not the Keo he once knew, but a Christian *and* a preacher in the Christian religion. Some voice, he says, told him to call Keo. There were no other immediate options.

That night, Kongkham struck a deal with his old friend, a kind of wager. "If you pray for my nephew," he told Keo over the phone, "and if everything turns out all right, then I will believe in your God."

Today, Kongkham and Vieng are both members of the Lao Unity Church; they were baptized little more than a week after the night their nephew nearly died but then returned to brimming health in a way, Kong believes, that could only be attributed to the God Pastor Keo called upon for a miracle. That night, that God delivered.

Kong's call caught Keo at a Bible study right there in the basement of the church. Sitting around the table with him were a number of Laotian Christians, studying God's word. When Keo reported on the call, all held hands and prayed for Ali. Not long afterward, the crisis passed and the boy took a turn for the better and lived.

Little more than a year has passed since that time. Not long ago, the people of the Lao Unity Church voted on who should be an elder, a leader among them. Kong was one of those chosen, even though he's only been a part of the fellowship for a year. The people respect him.

And today, he and Keo are together in a band once more, a

worship band that plays at every worship service. The music is different, of course. When worship is heartfelt, it is something of a party, of course — so what happens on Sunday in the Lao Unity church is a kind of party, but a world apart from the kind of parties they used to play.

"I don't listen to Buddha anymore," Kong says, "because I believe that God has called me — he's called me. Now I work for God, and I am happy because I am filled with him. I am born again," he says, and then this determined man smiles and breaks into a genial laugh.

And he and Khay Baccam, the familiar face he spotted in a grocery store, once a friend in the chaotic world of war-torn Laos, are today brothers in Christ. Today, in Sioux City, Iowa, United States of America, a world away from Vientiane, the old wartime friends are brothers in peace, the peace of the Lord Jesus Christ.

And one more little story — a kind of post script. The boy, Ali, he's just fine. He comes to church, too. Just thought you should know.

....

DOKMAI VONGPHAKDY

....

Crossing Over

Somewhere in their literature, all of the great religions of the world make use of the word picture embedded in the phrase *crossing over*. Something needs to be passed, needs to be crossed, needs to be taken on and overcome.

For Christians, the root of the word picture is the story of the recently freed Israelites approaching the Red Sea while being chased by legions of Egyptians, their former slave masters. For a moment, things looked hopeless. Then Moses prayed to the Lord and raised his hands, the waters separated, and the entire tribe marched through the miraculously dry riverbed.

Because an astonishing escape is at the heart of that tale, the phrase itself has come to mean much more than its reference to that great Old Testament story. With Christ as our Savior, we who name him as Lord can "cross over" this life and enter eternity with him.

The cross itself is a symbol of "crossing over"; Jesus Christ, who came to this earth to die for us, has given our lives here (the horizontal beam) eternal life above (the vertical beam). Jesus Christ, the God who became human, crossed over to bring us eternity with him.

But all of the great religions of the world use the idea of our need to pass beyond something that's limiting and thereby gain release and freedom and divine love. "Even if you were the worst of sinners," advises the Hindu scripture *Bhagavad Gita*, "you could cross beyond all sin by the raft of spiritual wisdom." And from the Buddhist *Dhammapada*: "Few are there among men who go across to the other shore; the rest of mankind only run about on the bank."

Vientiane

Dokmai Vongphakdy, who today lives in Sioux City, Iowa, has "crossed over." In her sixty-plus years (she's not sure exactly how old she is), she has crossed over the Mekong, not to mention the world itself and at least some of the world's great religious traditions. She is a believer, a Christian believer today, someone who puts her trust in the Lord Jesus Christ, someone who loves the Christian church where she worships so much that she says that she simply wants to be there all of the time.

Somewhere in the middle of her story is the most geographical "crossing over" of her life, her crossing the Mekong River, leaving Laos for Thailand after the communist takeover. Almost every Southeast Asian-American has a story of crossing over that river, and almost every story is different. Like many, Dokmai's crossing the Mekong doesn't lack for terrifying drama. But unlike many who were brimming with the excitement of new life on the other side, Dokmai wasn't so sure of herself when she crossed over, wasn't altogether confident that she was doing the right thing. In fact, her husband, who was already on the other side, had twice previously attempted to get her to escape. Twice, she had declined.

Dokmai was born into a poor, fatherless, and decimated family, her father dying when she was very young, so young that she has no memories at all of him. She was the youngest child of nine, several of whom had already died before she was old enough to understand what death meant. Her mother raised her in the city of Vientiane, where they farmed, which is to say, tried to grow enough food to stay alive. Her last surviving brother died when he was twelve and she was ten. He'd eaten bamboo he shouldn't have, went into convulsions, and did not recover.

The toll of sibling losses in her mother's family was unique, even to the neighbors. They were all spiritually driven people, of course, and a horrible phenomenon like the death of eight children was simply assumed to have spiritual causes. They consulted the shaman, the witch doctor, the spiritually enlightened man recognized for his ability to perceive and proclaim spiritual truth. He declared that to force the demons out and thereby save the life of Dokmai, the only surviving child, her mother should give up her last child. Dokmai remembers her mother weeping, but her mother did what she was told and sent her daughter to an aunt.

When Dokmai remembers that witch doctor's visit now — she was already fourteen years old — what she remembers best is how convincing he was. To prove his claim, he took out banana leaves and rubbed blisters that had formed on Dokmai's leg, then dropped those leaves in water. Dokmai saw it all. Magically, those leaves turned into eels, proof, the shaman said, that the evil spirit was already in Dokmai, that it was presently in her legs but would climb into her vital organs and eventually take her, too. Unless she left the home, she, like eight siblings before her, would be a victim of its evil.

In desperate times, faith may sometimes come a bit too easily.

Better times

Four years after Dokmai had gone to live with her aunt, another shaman told Dokmai's mother that the banana leaves test was a hoax and that the witch doctor simply wanted to pocket what little money she had. This second religious man told her mother that if she would give *him* the money, he would find a better way to dispose of the evil spirits. If she would pay him, she could have her daughter home again. Dokmai came home.

By that time, her mother had remarried. Things had begun to improve through their own hard work—turning Thai jungles into farmland, then planting and harvesting, and also fishing, then bringing what they could to market.

School? Really, there was nothing available, except for what little writing and reading she could pick up at the Buddhist temple on those nights her parents would attend. The only real need to learn, she says, was for her and her friends to be able to decipher the little notes boys would leave for the girls, little notes stuck in the sand near the well in the village, courting rituals she laughs to remember.

Life was improving significantly by that time, and Dokmai remembers knowing, and knowing well, that some children in the sprawling suburbs of Vientiane had far less to eat than she did. Her new family was not rich, but neither were they as poor as they had been.

At twenty-six, she was married. Her husband was a soldier, which meant that he attained a place of some prominence. But what she remembers of the time she had with him—only five years—is that more often than not he was off to wars that never seemed to cease. It wasn't the fighting that killed him, however; it was illness. While at the front, he became deeply ill. The army shipped him home, where he died, a man she still calls "her first love."

Five years passed. There were suitors, some of them too young, she says, and when she does she laughs as though the thought of them asking for her hand is silly now, years later. An older man, too, she remembers—too old. But she consented to one who came knocking, a man older than she was, a man with a trade, an electrician, a widower who was hunting somewhat feverishly. After all, he had six motherless children. What he needed, in many ways, was a woman.

In Dokmai's world, already difficult decisions were complicated greatly by their sheer necessity. When Dokmai considered the man's six children, the thought of marriage seemed daunting. But her parents agreed that it was the best thing to do; after all, the man was more than capable of providing a living, a handsome living. It was prudent to marry him. It wasn't that difficult to have six children, her stepfather told her; after all, they had maybe six dogs around the house where they lived. He told her there was likely little difference.

She married the electrician, and Dokmai, childless Dokmai, was instantly the mother of six.

"I really didn't want to get married to him," she says now, in part because of the pain of losing that first love. But this man had money—he could provide. There were real benefits in her marrying him. Her will in this relationship was simply not as important as the needs of the family. She married the electrician, and Dokmai, childless Dokmai, was instantly the mother of six.

Crossing the Mekong

For several years, the new relationship was difficult; the demands of rearing his children at times seemed more than Dokmai could take. Then she got pregnant herself; she was, by then, forty-something. First, a son was born, then, a year later, a girl. And in that time, she says today, she began to understand how to love this man she'd married—and he began to understand her. That's the way she puts it.

Meanwhile, simply staying alive was becoming easier. Sufficient food was there for the growing family, and work was plentiful. But then the communists came, and when her husband decided that he didn't want to go off to a forced labor camp, he left for Thailand, a refugee. He left alone, without her, something that happened frequently back then.

When two of his sons returned for Dokmai—and it was, of course, dangerous to steal their way back into Laos—she said no. She wasn't anxious to "cross over," and her stepfather opposed her leaving. "Even if people say the Americans will help the refugee people," he told her, "you must remember that we have been poor. If you go, things could well get worse for us." As always, *family* needed to be considered. She listened to her stepfather and stayed behind with the two children she'd had with the electrician, the man who'd already left.

But what happened under communist rule eventually changed her stepfather's mind. He decided that the communist way of doing things—all of them working together—didn't promise great happiness for any of them. Furthermore, he worried that she might be led, in her husband's absence, to marry someone else, someone who wouldn't love her children as the electrician had. Reluctantly, he told her finally to go.

When she did cross the Mekong, she was on her own; neither her stepsons nor her husband were there to guide her. A cousin had experience leading people across the Mekong, and he told his family that he was going to do it again, this time for the last time. Such trips were perilous, and there had to be a better life somewhere. Then he asked Dokmai if she wanted to leave, and, with her stepfather's blessing, she decided that crossing over was the best thing to do.

Her son was seven and her daughter five when, on the night of their departure, they waited until darkness at the edge of the city, waited until there was no sign of the communist soldiers who regularly policed the river. It was raining, pouring, which was a blessing, keeping those who would keep them from crossing over somewhere under cover.

Other stories of crossing over include gunfire; others include sadness and horror. What Dokmai remembers is hanging on to the little boat they stole before leaving—a tiny, narrow, canoe-like skiff which held little more than her two children. The adults—Dokmai, an aunt, two cousins, and another man, all family—held on to the side as they swam, the kids sitting inside, rain pouring down. They'd planned to use a tire, a tube, as a float across the water; but when the opportunity for that little boat came along, they grabbed it, tossed the tube inside, and started swimming.

What they discovered was that their seemingly good fortune had holes, plenty of them. The adults held on to the side, wading when they could, swimming when they had to, while the Mekong itself was rising inside. She remembers — she'll never forget — telling her kids to bail, bail, bail, to empty the water that was coming from beneath and above, the sky itself full of rain.

Two hours after leaving their home, they were in Thailand. And all through this crossing over, all through her life for that matter, Dokmai remembers praying, praying fervently to a God she claims that she didn't **Over and over again, she remembers, she told them to pray, pray, pray.** know at that time, a God whose outline and story were not at all familiar to her, the God of the universe, whoever that might be, the God who simply had to be there, listening to all of the prayers of all of the people who needed him. If anything, she'll say, it was something like the Buddhist god. All she knew then, she says, is that she pleaded for his blessing.

When the rain came down and the boat rode low in the water, when the depth was farther than her feet could reach, all she could do, she says, is pray, for herself and for the precious cargo bailing away as fast as they could. And she told her children to pray. Over and over again, she remembers, she told them to pray, pray, pray.

On the Mekong, most stories of crossing over don't end with immediate joy and happiness once the refugees wash up on the opposite shore. For many, the danger they'd thought behind them grew only worse when people who cared nothing for their plight robbed them of everything, including, often enough, their own precious human dignity. Rape and murder were not infrequent.

Guardian angel

What Dokmai Vongphakdy remembers about her crossing over is how they arrived when it was dangerously dark, three in the morning, how dogs barked at their unwelcome presence, how she and her refugee family members walked toward the tomato gardens of whoever lived along the river in Thailand, and how, finally, once it was light, they pleaded for their lives with a man who found them. "Oh, please, do not shoot us," she sobbed. "We are Laotians, escaping, and we have children. Please do not shoot us."

The man stopped. He made no move. This man — the first man they met — asked them if they had money. If they didn't, he said, he was going to tell the Thai soldiers to arrest them.

"Please," she pleaded, "we are neighbors — we are brothers and sisters. We are separated from our husbands. Please help us."

Miraculously, as if he were an appointed angel, he did.

She showed him what money she'd carried along. Today, twenty years later, Dokmai Vongphakdy scolds herself for her foolishness, for her naiveté. "I showed all my money to the man and he didn't take it," she says. But he told her never to risk that again.

He paid for their bus tickets himself, this guardian angel. Then he asked Dokmai if she could speak Thai. She told him only Lao-Thai, a kind of hybrid of the two languages. "That's not good enough," he told her. "When you're on the bus," he said, "just keep your mouth shut, no matter what." Otherwise, he said, they could be arrested. Then he told them to hide their money and even showed them where, in her little boy's shoes.

Through all of this, you remember, she was praying to a God she didn't know, praying fervently, without ceasing. It appears, however, whether or not she knew him, that God Almighty certainly knew her; because this man — the man who stumbled upon them when they crossed over, he was, without a doubt, a blessing.

For many reasons, including some impossible even to imagine from North America, life in the camp at Napoo, where they stayed, was hardly a joy. She'd undertaken this escape without her husband's knowledge, of course, and he was surprised when suddenly she showed up. He had already taken up with another woman, and he threatened her life when first he saw her again. With her children, she was alone.

And she had nothing. Because many other refugees were already receiving money from relatives who'd made it to the States, she was, for a time, among the poorest of the poor in the camp at Napoo. It became her lot to do almost anything anyone of higher standing demanded she would do. This particular story of "crossing over" does not have a heavenly ending.

Despite his threats, she told her husband that she was not going to leave Napoo, that if he didn't want her anymore that was okay. But she also told him that if he wanted her back, she would still be his wife, and he could still be the father of their two children. At first, he raged and spit and fumed. In three weeks, however, he moved back with her again.

Meanwhile, she had been taken in by another guardian angel, someone in authority in the camp, who gave her work in his house. Soon, when she was reunited with her husband, her work and his meant they were no longer at the bottom in the camp, no longer hungry. Yet, when she remembers Napoo today, she says she is simply sad. "I want to cry because it was so dangerous," she says, dangerous especially for her children.

This new faith

As it was for many others, her introduction to Christianity occurred in the camp. At the beginning, the Christian faith seemed to her to be little more than a synonym for "help." If you needed something, you go to the Christians. If you wanted to get out of the camp more quickly, you go to the Christians. If you had to have something that you couldn't get elsewhere, you go to the Christians. She knew next to nothing about the faith, only that the Christians were the source of aid. That's what everyone said, and it was true.

But she couldn't. Someone said, "Mother, don't you want to go to church? If you go, they'll help you with many things."

"Who will take care of my children?" she said. "Who will

watch them?"

Through all of this, she kept on praying. "In my situation," she says today, "I always felt close to God. I would call to God, the Buddhist god, but I didn't know him, didn't know what he looked like at all. I had a relationship with something, maybe a spirit." That's the way she sees it today.

When finally the day arrived for the next crossing over, her trip to America, she was, once again, ambivalent. Her husband had his heart set on leaving; two of his sons were already working in a place called Sioux City, Iowa. But her heart, as it had so often been, was with her own family.

This is what her stepfather said. "You should go," he told her, "because if we don't die, I know we will see each other again."

With that assurance and that blessing, she and her husband and their own two children left Napoo and Laos and Southeast Asia.

The land of no bowing

What she remembers best of those first few days in America is a trip to a supermarket. She claims it took her an entire day to walk through and see everything, an entire day, like an awestruck child in a candy store. When white people would smile at her, she says, she simply assumed that they liked her.

She knew no English, of course, so before she found a regular job, she tried to get any kind of work she could to support her family. At first, when she'd be warmly greeted, she'd walk up to whoever had smiled and tug at the ends of her sleeves, trying to indicate that she would appreciate the opportunity to wash clothes. One man—a neighbor—interpreted the gesture in a wholly different way and brought over a number of shirts. She laughs now when she thinks of it.

This man, another guardian angel, took an interest in her, gave her food, looked out for her interest, even brought her to church. And when he did, she showed her respect and appreciation for what he did in the only way she knew: she bowed to him, hands together, as if in prayer.

"No," he told her, pulling her to her feet. "You're in America now — no bowing."

It seems almost silly to her now to remember how little she knew or understood about this whole new world.

This man, she says, this neighbor, "became a little like family to me. He was a friend, and I would do anything for him."

In a month or so, she had herself a job at Iowa Beef Processors, just as her husband and his sons. They were all at IBP.

What she remembers best of those first few days in America is a trip to a supermarket.

In a way what's amazing about Dokmai's story is that all this "crossing over," from motherless child to loving daughter, from sweetheart to widow, from childless wife to mother of six, from Laos to Thailand, from Thailand to America, from refugee to contributing member of a whole new society, from scorned to beloved — what's amazing about the whole story is that all of this crossing over was accomplished with what seems to be so little trauma. Today, Dokmai pages through the story of her own life as though what happened to her were not at all extraordinary. What remains on her face throughout the whole story is some kind of steadfast smile.

Church

There is no startling moment in her pilgrimage to faith in Jesus Christ, no sudden light on the road, no angel any more resplendent than those who'd come to her aid when she needed it on the banks of the Mekong and in the neighborhood where she lived when she first came to Sioux City, Iowa. For some time after those first years in the States, like so many others, she attended church regularly, even used the church to gain citizenship. "But I didn't understand anything about the Lord Jesus Christ," she says, even though the services were in the Lao tongue. She never really got it, never under-stood, never really took home a sense of what it meant to be a believer in Christ.

What helped greatly was the influence of her pastor, Keo Phommarath, a man she'd known before he'd become a be-liever, and a man whose whole life changed dramatically, mi-raculously, before her eyes when he came to see his need for a Savior. It was Keo's influence, the Bible studies she attended and the worship services she frequented, that made her come to understand what it was that lay at the heart of the Christian gospel, that helped her identify, really, who it was she was praying to all of her life. "Now I feel like everything that hap-pened in my life, all the bad things, was all part of the Lord's plan for me," she says, "and now I am happy."

Her husband, the electrician, is gone. His wandering, back in Laos, didn't stop when he came to Sioux City. They were divorced six years ago.

But that steadfast smile re-mains. "I feel the Holy Spirit in me. He made preaching and Bible study really make sense," she says. "And when I saw the people in the church, and their lives—the Holy Spirit used that for me, too."

Sadness, but no despair

Even though she is alone, she says she is in "a perfect posi-tion right now." She says she wants and needs to be a good Christian for her children; they are not believers—yet. But there's far too much behind her for her to feel any resignation or despair. She knows not only how long people can wander in darkness before they see a great light, but also how this God, the Father of Jesus Christ, can be relentless in his pursuit of those he loves.

"In my heart, I am feeling happiness with the Lord Jesus and God," she says. "I just want to be at the church all the time because it makes me so happy. I would sleep here if I could."

Dokmai has crossed over so often in her life that, to most of us, the difficulties she's suffered and the changes she's endured seem unimaginable. But she's arrived—that much she knows.

The love she feels is so great that it has become her task to minister to her children's faithlessness. And her parents'. On either generational side of her life, there remains unbelief. "I think about my family back in Laos," she says, "and I want so badly to go back home and tell them the Good News. I'm praying for them, and I'm going to keep on being with the Lord."

Dokmai Vongphakdy has crossed over and, thanks be to God, she's arrived.

....

Printed in the United States
72111LV00004B/232-282

9 780932 914675